FYI FOR TALENT MANAGEMENT™
THE TALENT DEVELOPMENT HANDBOOK

ROBERT W. EICHINGER
MICHAEL M. LOMBARDO
CARA CAPRETTA RAYMOND

The LEADERSHIP ARCHITECT® is the exclusive registered
trademark of Lominger Limited, Inc.
www.lominger.com

item number 61031

first printing 5-04
second printing 10-04

ISBN 0-9745892-2-5

TABLE OF CONTENTS

THE TALENT DEVELOPMENT HANDBOOK

Talent is usually considered the people who are in the upper 10 percent of what they do. What separates the best from the rest who perform well? To be good at anything requires some knowledge, skills, and technical know how. Both the best and the rest have that. One thing that separates the best from the rest is the ability to adjust, adapt, respond to, and be resourceful in the face of change. You could call it "performing well under first-time conditions." How well do you do if you have never done exactly that before? This ability to take meaning from the past and fit it to something different is one of the things that separates the best from the rest. In this handbook we present tips and strategies to help people reach the top 10 percent in learning agility.

Regardless of how intelligent or technically skilled you are, the best way to increase your talent score or effectiveness is to improve your learning agility. Relatively unrelated to intelligence (also good to have), learning agility is basically how well you adapt to the new and different. An increasing number of studies show that:

- ☐ Learning agility is more predictive of level attained or career ladder achievement in an organization than intelligence.

- ☐ Learning agility is highly related to being labeled as a so-called high potential.

- ☐ Once promoted, people with higher learning agility perform significantly better than those with lower learning agility.

- ☐ Learning agility matters just as much for individual contributors as it does for managers and executives, males and females, line and staff roles.

- ☐ It is unrelated to how old you are.

WHAT IS LEARNING AGILITY?

A major characteristic of successful people at any level and any age is being a learner—actively making sense of work and personal experiences, adding those lessons to their lifelong learnings portfolio, and striving to get better. Learning new job and technical knowledge (have to be able to do) is different from learning new personal and managerial behavior or ways of viewing events and problems. Changing beliefs, attitudes, values, and behaviors is different than learning a new technical skill or learning about a new industry. People high in learning agility learn to act and behave differently.

In multi-year studies conducted at the Center for Creative Leadership, one of the glaring differences between successful executives and those whose careers, although successful in the early years, go into eclipse (they derail) is their agility in wresting meaning from experience. Successful executives are much more likely to have active and numerous learning strategies. They learn faster, gaining their lessons closer to on-the-spot, not because they are more intelligent, but because they have more learning skills and strategies that help them learn what to do when they don't know what to do. They are also more open to what they don't know. They are energized by the challenge of learning how to do something better and differently.

In contrast, derailed, less successful managers tend to learn randomly or not at all. Their lessons either form no pattern or are vague pronouncements without much meat to them. They are not active learners who seek to make sense of their experiences, searching for learning that might be applicable in the future. They are not energized by not knowing something.

WHY IS LEARNING AGILITY SO IMPORTANT IN BUILDING TALENT?

Because we're creatures of habit, we rely on successful habits from the past, and under the pressures of change or new situations, we have a natural tendency to stick to our comfort zone and repeat what has worked for us previously. Learning agility helps us get out of our ruts, learn something new, and do something different—responding to change instead of just responding to demands to change.

People who learn lessons of work and life faster aren't any smarter from a raw intelligence standpoint. They simply have more learning strategies in their arsenal to help them learn what to do when what they've been doing isn't working as well.

WHAT IS THE BEST STRATEGY TO INCREASE LEARNING AGILITY?

You can do three things. You can improve, use substitutes, or use workarounds.

Improvement Strategies

You can work to improve. You can work on your weak areas that are mission critical to what you do. We recommend a six-pronged strategy:

1. Find and use your learning strengths. Find your highest Factor (there are four, see below) or cluster of Dimensions (there are 27 learning themes) and leverage them. If you excel at seeing problems differently, get into more situations that allow you to hone your strengths.
2. Neutralize your weaker learning areas. If you're not terribly personable or hate to deal with conflict, your first goal should be to turn this from a negative to a neutral. Start small, using the tips in this talent development guide.
3. Seek further feedback. Little happens without feedback tied to a goal. Get a developmental partner, get feedback a year from now on CHOICES ARCHITECT® 2nd Edition, ask for an INTERVIEW ARCHITECT® Learning From Experience (LFE) interview, poll people you work with about what you should keep doing, keep doing with slight modifications, stop doing, and start doing.
4. Test the unknown. Many learning dimensions you might be low on reflect lack of experience that we call an untested area. Maybe you don't deal with change well, but have never led a change

effort. Pick something small that needs doing, and give it a try using the tips on Change Agility.

5. Go against your natural grain. We call these GAG (going against your natural grain). GAG because it is uncomfortable. If you're ambitious or if you seek a different kind of job, you'll have to work on your downsides more vigorously than the suggestion in number 2 above. Few succeed in a different job by simply repeating past successful behavior. This is a strong lesson from career research. You'll have to stretch in uncomfortable areas. For example, whether you gravitate toward team building or not, you can learn the behaviors of excellent team builders. You might even come to enjoy it. It's important not to confuse what you like to do with what's necessary to do.

6. You don't have to be good at everything. Most successful leaders have four to six major strengths but tend to lack glaring weaknesses. Developing in all 27 Dimensions of CHOICES is unlikely. Use the strategies above to select wisely.

If directly working on improvement is not useful at the moment, use the two indirect strategies of substitution and workaround:

Substitution Strategies

Use an existing strength to substitute for a weakness. This path requires using a current strength to neutralize a weakness. Here are a few examples of how you could substitute a strength to attack a weakness in presentation skills.

1. Upgrade the use of humor (already a high skill) in your presentations. Using cartoons and humorous dialogue would increase audience acceptance and lead to a higher evaluation of the success of the presentation even though basic presentation skills would not have been improved.

2. Facilitate (already a high skill) instead of present. Minimize presentation time and increase discussion and audience participation.

3. Tape portions of the presentation where you could rehearse, do multiple takes, and insert taped portions into the live presentation.

4. Write (already a high skill) out your points and distribute them ahead of the meeting and then have a discussion instead of making a speech.

Again, the outcome is to reduce the impact of being a marginal presenter by substituting things you are already good at to get the same thing done. This approach is relatively easy to do if you have the strengths necessary to counter your need.

Substitutes are many times found in the same Factor as the need. So first look to the other Dimensions in the same Factor to see if one of your strengths might be used as a substitute.

Substitutes are also listed in 4th Edition *FYI For Your Improvement*™. Using the competency map in each chapter, look to the competencies that are most associated with your need and look to the substitutes to see if you have any of those strengths.

Workaround Strategies

Work around the weakness. This involves using other resources to get the same thing done. While there may or may not be any learning attached to the workaround, this gets done what has to be done without directly addressing the personal need. Essential to this approach is self-knowledge. You have to know you have the need and acknowledge its importance. Some general workaround tips follow.

GENERAL WORKAROUND TIPS

As with the other strategies, the goal of a workaround is to reduce the noise caused by having the need. What follows is a general workaround list of tips that would apply to many different weaknesses or needs:

People workarounds...

Find an internal person to stand in for you when the weakness is in play. A peer. An internal consultant. A friend. A person from your staff.

So if you are a marginal presenter, get someone who is a good presenter to present your material.

Find an external person to stand in for you when the weakness is in play. This is usually a consultant who specializes in doing what you are not good at. If you are marginal on strategic thinking, hire a consultant or a firm who creates strategic plans you can choose from.

Hire people for your team who are good in the areas you are not. Delegate the tasks that bring the weakness into play.

Task workarounds...

Trade tasks with a peer. Trade for something you are good at and trade away the task you are struggling with. You help a peer with his or her strategic planning and he or she helps you with your presentations to senior management.

Share tasks. Partner with someone to combine tasks and share so that each of you does the tasks you are best at.

Structure the weakness out. Redesign your job (with your boss) so that you are not responsible for the task(s) that brings your weakness into play. Change your job so that you no longer have to give lots of speeches to strangers. Assign that task to another unit.

Change workarounds...

Change jobs (companies, units, divisions). If you decide that you don't want to work on your needs, do an honest assessment of your strengths and find an organization, a job, or another unit that fits those strengths. You are in sales and you are good at everything but cold calling and lead generation. Find a sales job where leads are provided or customers come to you.

Change careers. If you decide that you don't want to address this need, do an honest assessment of your strengths and find a different career that does not call upon your areas of weakness but instead requires the portfolio of strengths you do have. If you are in sales promotion and are not a comfortable presenter or cold caller, then consider marketing analysis where those two requirements are greatly decreased.

Self workarounds...

Pre-declare your weakness. Research shows that admitting weaknesses (within limits) actually increase people's evaluations of you. So if you start by saying, "As most of you know, speaking is not one of my strengths," people will not be as critical.

Redefine yourself. Live with it. If you decide not to address the need, concentrate harder on the things you do well.

WHAT DO PEOPLE WITH HIGH LEARNING AGILITY LOOK LIKE?

People high in learning agility do four things well:

1. They are critical thinkers who examine problems carefully and make fresh connections.

2. They know themselves better and are able to handle tough people situations deftly.

3. They like to experiment and can deal with the discomfort that surrounds change.

4. They deliver results in first-time situations through team building and personal drive.

THE KEY CHARACTERISTICS OF HIGH LEARNERS ARE:

1. Mental Agility
Curious
Get to root causes
Comfortable with complexity and ambiguity
Find parallels and contrasts
Question conventional wisdom
Find solutions to tough problems
Read broadly

2. People Agility
Open-minded
Self-aware
Personal improver
Comfortable with diversity
Can play many roles
Understand others
Like to help others succeed
Politically agile
Have a light touch
Deal with conflict constructively
Skilled communicator

3. Change Agility
Tinkerer
Can take the heat
Introduce new slants

4. Results Agility
Build high-performing teams
Can pull off things against the odds
Have drive and personal presence
Very flexible and adaptable

ORGANIZATION OF FYI FOR TALENT MANAGEMENT™

Each of the 27 chapters follow this format:

1. **Definition**—What Skilled and Unskilled look like for this Dimension of learning agility. As all Dimensions lie in one of four CHOICES ARCHITECT® 2nd Edition Factors, we include a High and Low definition of the Factor as well so you can put the Dimension into context. This precedes the first Dimension in each Factor.

2. **The specific Items** in CHOICES used to measure this Dimension.

3. **A map to the LEADERSHIP ARCHITECT® Competencies**—This indicates which of the 67 Competencies in the library are either strongly, moderately, or lightly related to this Dimension. With the map, you could compare a person who has had 360° feedback against the Dimension. Also, using the map, you could study more remedies in the *FYI For Your Improvement*™ book.

4. **Some Causes**—We list numerous reasons why you might have this need. Use these to specify what your need looks like exactly. What causes a need might be very different for each individual. The difference might lead to quite different remedies. You might not listen because you are very impatient with everything and everyone. You just don't take the time to listen. On the other hand, you might not listen because you don't think anyone else is smarter than you are. Or you might not listen because you avoid feedback and are very defensive. Even though the weakness is the same—you don't listen—the underlying cause is quite different and the fix or remedy will be completely different.

5. **The Map**—This gives you the general lay of the land. It reviews the general case of the Dimension, how it operates, and why it is important. It puts the Dimension into context.

6. **Some Remedies**—At least 10 tips are included to work directly on this need. Although a few may be longer term, most are things you can start working on today. For each Dimension, we include one or more workarounds, if you decide to take an indirect route to working on the need.

7. **More Help?** For those who have a copy of *FYI For Your Improvement*™, we include 10 tips for each of the items measuring this Dimension.

8. **Jobs**—Most development of learning agility takes place when it has to, under challenging job conditions. Lots of people pause at this section. Why have a job in here? I already have a job or I don't want to do this one or it would be risky for me to get in such a job (e.g., a strategic planning job when I'm lousy at making connections). If this is your last job or you have no career ambition to do anything different or at a higher level, skip this section. Otherwise read on.

   This section is here because:
   - The number one developer of competence by far is stretching, challenging jobs—not feedback, not courses, not role models, but jobs where you develop and exercise significant and varied competencies. If you really want to grow, these are the best places to do it.
   - If you are ambitious, these are the jobs that matter most for long-term success. In the CCL studies, executives who remained successful had been tested in many of the jobs you'll see in this section.
   - You have a rich opportunity to use your job to learn better from experience. What specifically about the job demands that you work on this need? Write down these challenges; focus your development on them.

9. **Part-Time Assignments**—Unless you have challenging job tasks where you either perform against the need or fail, not much development will occur. This is the essence of action learning or learning from experience—not practice, not trying things out, but getting better in order to perform. Take the example of listening skills, a common need. Everyone has had a million chances (practices) to listen better but they don't, usually because there are some people or some situations where they don't want to listen and have gotten away with it. To listen better, then, how about if they were in a tough negotiation or running a task force

of experts when they're not an expert. Get the idea? It's listen or else you can't do the job. It's listen or fail. Any plan you write must have "perform this or else" tasks in it to work. Otherwise you'll revert to your old ways. To use these tasks, shape them to your job and organization. What tasks like these are available? If you have a significant need (you are really weak in this area), start with smaller challenges and build up to the tougher ones.

10. **Suggested Readings.** We have added hundreds of books, Web sites and audiotapes to help you go beyond the tips we present in these pages. Each of the 27 chapters in *FYI for Talent Management*™ has 10 to 20 sources for further reading or listening.

   ### We used these selection criteria:

   - ROI—Is there a significant and immediate payoff for reading this book? Are there suggestions busy people can implement?
   - Organization—Is the book well laid out? Is it easy to find what you are looking for?
   - Ease—Is it well written?
   - Solid—Is the advice more than opinion?
   - Prolific—Are there lots of tips and examples?
   - Available—Can the book (or audiotape) be found without a search?

   To insure that the books were solid, we relied heavily on the Library Journal, which reviews and recommends the best business books every year. So the books are substantive and mostly available through your local public library.

Second, we relied on Soundview, so many of the books would be conveniently available in eight-page summaries. Soundview Executive Book Summaries, 10 LaCrue Avenue, Concordville, PA 19331. 1-800-521-1227. International calls outside the U.S. and Canada 1-610-558-9495. (www.summary.com) We also used 24x7, a subscription service, to access and read books online. The service provides a summary as well as links to the actual book content. (www.books24x7.com)

Third, we checked major booksellers (Amazon, Barnes & Noble, B. Dalton, Borders) to see what they stock. In general, they are similar in coverage to Soundview.

Finally, we checked MBA syllabi to see what universities regard as substantive for business people.

So increasing your talent quotient starts with an assessment of the Dimensions of learning agility. You can do this with a self-assessment tool like the one in the back of this book. Unfortunately, this approach is probably the least accurate. Better would be to have both you and your boss fill out the assessment, then compare results. You could also talk through the Dimensions with your boss or mentor, get CHOICES feedback (CHOICES measures the 27 Dimensions of learning agility), be interviewed by someone certified in the INTERVIEW ARCHITECT® Learning From Experience (LFE) technique, or you can compare your VOICES® 360° feedback report with the LEADERSHIP ARCHITECT® Competency map in each Dimension chapter.

Once you have a pattern of your strengths and weaknesses, how matched are you with your current situation? How do you fit with the next thing you want to do? Which weaknesses are now or are going to be mission critical? Then decide which path you are going to follow—improve, substitute, or workaround. A full attack might be to pick actions that substitute instantly and use workarounds for the short term, all the while trying to actively improve.

ABOUT THE AUTHORS

Bob Eichinger has over 40 years experience in management and executive development. He held executive development positions at PepsiCo and Pillsbury and has consulted with hundreds of organizations on succession planning and development. He has lectured extensively on the topic of executive and management development and has served on the Board of the Human Resource Planning Society, a professional association of people charged with the responsibility of management and executive development in their organizations. Along with Mike Lombardo and others, Bob has written several books and articles and created over 20 paper and software products for helping people grow and develop.

Mike Lombardo has over 20 years experience in executive and management research and in executive coaching. He is one of the founders of Lominger Limited, Inc., publishers of the LEADERSHIP ARCHITECT® Suite. With Bob Eichinger, Mike has authored 20 products for the suite, including *The Leadership Machine*, *FYI For Your Improvement*™, the CAREER ARCHITECT®, CHOICES ARCHITECT®, and VOICES®. During his 15 years at the Center for Creative Leadership, Mike was a co-author of *The Lessons of Experience*, which detailed which learnings from experience can teach the competencies needed to be successful. He also co-authored the research on executive derailment revealing how personal flaws and overdone strengths caused otherwise effective executives to get into career trouble, BENCHMARKS®, a 360° feedback instrument; and the LOOKING GLASS® simulation. Mike has won four national awards for research on managerial and executive development.

 Cara Capretta Raymond is Vice President of Product and Business Development for Lominger Limited, Inc. She is the co-author of *FYI for Teams*, a book for developing entire teams, team members and team leaders, and co-author of *The Interview Architect*, a book for developing competency-based interview guides. Cara has nearly 15 years of practical experience working with leaders, teams and organizations on development. Prior to joining Lominger, she was the Director of Executive Development for Nationwide, a Fortune 500 insurance company, where she designed and implemented a succession planning system to identify, develop and place global talent in an organization with over 30,000 employees.

HIGH

People high on this Factor are oriented toward newness and complexity and are described as mentally quick. They are seen as curious and inquisitive. They like to delve deeply into problems, thoroughly analyzing them through contrasts, parallels, and searching for meaning. They can get to the essence of issues better than most others can. Additionally, they can help other people think things through.

LOW

People low on this Factor may have gotten stale. They may be caught in present paradigms, may be uncomfortable with change, ambiguity, and things that are messy and uncertain. Being oriented to known solutions, they may hop from solution to solution when a nasty problem appears rather than reexamining the issue for a fresh perspective. As such, they probably focus on **what**, not **why and how**, and don't search either their personal history or relevant parallels to a great degree. They may have trouble explaining how they arrived at a position and, as a consequence, might appear biased, non-objective, or even arbitrary in their positions and solutions. They many not be able to articulate the positions of others.

SOME CAUSES

☐ Arrogant

☐ Doesn't listen

☐ Impatient

☐ Inconsistent

☐ Low comfort with uncertainty

continued

1

- [ ] Mentally lazy
- [ ] Narrow background
- [ ] Not orderly
- [ ] Opinionated
- [ ] Overly biased against others
- [ ] Relies on the past
- [ ] Too focused
- [ ] Too rigid/stuck in their ways
- [ ] Too specialized

Factor I

DIMENSION 1
BROAD SCANNER

SKILLED
Very knowledgeable on a host of work and non-work topics.

UNSKILLED
May use limited sources or limited media for knowledge.

ITEMS
- ☐ 1. Reads broadly.
- ☐ 28. Uses history and biography to find common truths, rules, and how things work.
- ☐ 55. Knows a lot about many work and non-work topics.

LEADERSHIP ARCHITECT® COMPETENCIES MOST ASSOCIATED WITH THIS DIMENSION

Strong
- ☐ 32. Learning on the Fly
- ☐ 46. Perspective

Moderate
- ☐ 2. *Dealing with* Ambiguity
- ☐ 51. Problem Solving
- ☐ 62. Time Management

Light
- ☐ 33. Listening
- ☐ 52. Process Management
- ☐ 54. Self-Development

SOME CAUSES

☐ Doesn't take time to learn

☐ Doesn't value information not needed now

☐ Impatient

☐ Intimidated by information technology

☐ Life partner(s) also specialized or narrow

☐ Low curiosity

☐ Low tolerance for complexity

☐ Low tolerance for uncertainty

☐ Narrow band of friends, acquaintances

☐ Narrow or limited interests

☐ Prefers depth to broad

☐ Too busy

☐ Too specialized

☐ Uncomfortable approaching others for information

THE MAP

In several studies, those with a broad scope were more successful than those with a more narrow scope. A broad scope gives us more chances to come up with meaningful connections to our life and work, and ideas don't originate from boxes labeled "directly relevant to my life right this minute." Our minds are more flexible than this. Those with a broad view offer more.

SOME REMEDIES

☐ 1. Select a biography of a historical figure you admire but don't know much about. What made the figure significant? What were his or her key accomplishments and contributions? What were critical lessons in his or her life? Write down five things you can emulate in your own behavior. A helpful Web site for finding biographical summaries, books, videos, etc. is

4

www.biography.com. Additionally, they list a monthly schedule for the Biography Channel, a cable channel on the A&E network dedicated to biography shows and specials on significant lives.

☐ 2. Pick three books on topics you don't know much about and write down three things for each that relate to your job and life.

☐ 3. Start reading periodicals such as the *Economist, New Yorker, Atlantic Monthly, Forbes, Fortune,* and *BusinessWeek.* Keep a log of ideas you get from each.

☐ 4. Go remote: Read a philosopher, a religious tract, or a book about physics written for the layperson. Ask yourself what common truths or insights you can gain about human nature, the way things work, and about yourself.

☐ 5. Use the Internet to understand world events from other perspectives. Read the Russian view of the Middle East, what drives the French economy, how Turkey controls the water supply to many countries. Use these primarily for personal perspective but secondarily for understanding differences.

☐ 6. Learn more about your business. Talk to the people who know. Meet with the strategic planners, and read every significant document you can find about your business, it's customers and competitors. Reduce your understanding to rules of thumb and use these to image what initiative could make a huge difference.

☐ 7. Spend time socially or at work (lunches, outings) with those who are broad in viewpoint and diverse in background. Pay attention to topics they discuss that you aren't versed in. Make a point to learn or discover new information from them. Consider researching or investigating those topics afterward to learn more so that you can converse with them at the next encounter.

☐ 8. Attend broadening workshops and lectures on topics you normally don't get exposed to often.

☐ 9. **(Workaround)** Seek counsel and advice from those broader than you.

☐ 10. **(Workaround)** Use an internal or external consultant to study the broadest aspects of issues and challenges you are facing and offer input you might want to consider.

MORE HELP?

See *FYI For Your Improvement*™. We have coded each item to about 10 tips from the *FYI* book. To use this resource, the codes below refer to the chapter and then the tip number from the *FYI* book. For example, in item 1 below, 2-3 refers to Chapter 2—*Dealing with Ambiguity*, tip 3. If you don't have a copy of *FYI*, it is available through Lominger at 952-345-3610 or www.lominger.com

1. Reads broadly.
2-3; 30-10; 46-1,2,3,5,6; 58-3,6; 118-8

28. Uses history and biography to find common truths, rules, and how things work.
14-2; 30-10; 32-2,3; 46-1,2,3,6; 58-3,6

55. Knows a lot about many work and non-work topics.
5-6; 9-1; 24-1; 28-10; 32-5,7; 46-5,7,8; 66-6

JOBS THAT WOULD ADD SKILLS IN THIS DIMENSION

☐ Cross Moves—across functions/SBU's/products/services.

☐ Out of Home Country Assignments—where you have to make the connection between your background and this new setting.

☐ Scope (very broad) Assignments—often involving new businesses, functions to deal with. Requires making a significant transition, such as to manager of managers or functional head to general manager.

PART-TIME ASSIGNMENTS THAT WOULD ADD SKILLS IN THIS DIMENSION

☐ Assemble a team of diverse people to accomplish a difficult task.

☐ Integrate systems, processes, or procedures across decentralized and/or dispersed units.

☐ Work on a project that involves travel to places you have never been to or study issues you have never studied.

☐ Study a new trend, product, service, technique, or process you have never experienced before.

☐ Manage a project team made up of nationals from a number of countries you have not had any experience with before.

☐ Study the history of an event or an institution or country you have had no experience with before.

SUGGESTED READINGS

Atlantic Monthly. http://www.theatlantic.com

BusinessWeek. http://www.businessweek.com

Collins, J. *Good to great.* New York: Harper Collins, 2001.

Commentary Magazine. http://www.commentarymagazine.com

Drucker, P. *Management challenges for the 21st century.* New York: HarperBusiness, 1999.

Dudik, E. *Strategic renaissance.* New York: AMACOM, 2000.

Economist. http://www.economist.com

Futurist Magazine. http://www.wfs.org

Gibbon, Edward. *History of the decline and fall of the Roman Empire.* A modern abridgment by Moses Hadas. New York: Putnam, 1962.

Green, Peter. *Alexander of Macedon, 356–323 B.C. A historical biography.* Los Angeles: University of California Press, 1991.

Hamel, Gary. *Leading the revolution.* Watertown, MA: Harvard Business School Press, 2000.

Hamel, Gary and C.K. Prahalad. *Competing for the future.* Boston, MA: Harvard Business School Press, 1994.

Harvard Business Review. Mail: Harvard Business Review, Subscriber Services, P.O. Box 52623, Boulder, CO 80322-2623 USA. Phone: 800-988-0886 (U.S. and Canada). Fax: 617-496-1029. http://www.hbsp.harvard.edu/products/hbr

International Herald Tribune. http://www.iht.com

Kennedy, Paul M. *The rise and fall of the great powers: Economic change and military conflict from 1500 to 2000.* New York: Random House, 1987.

Porter, Michael E. *On competition.* Boston: Harvard Business School Press, 1998.

Sloan Management Review. Cambridge, MA: Industrial Management Review Association at the Alfred P. Sloan School of Management, Massachusetts Institute of Technology. http://mitsloan.mit.edu/smr

Soundview Executive Book Summaries. 10 LaCrue Avenue, Concordville, PA 19331. Phone: 800-521-1227. 1-610-558-9495 (outside U.S. and Canada). http://www.summary.com (Soundview Executive Book Summaries are 5,000-word, eight-page distillations of specially selected business books. Soundview subscribers receive two or three eight-page Summaries of the best business books each month [30 per year], access to well over 200 Summaries on Soundview's backlist, and access to editors in Soundview's research department for help in finding specific business book references.)

Strategic Leadership Forum. 230 E. Ohio Street, Suite 400, Chicago, IL 60611-4067. 800-873-5995 Fax: 312-644-8557. http://www.slfnet.org

Wall Street Journal. http://www.wsj.com

SKILLED

Comfortable with things that don't fit; casts a broad net; doesn't try to make things simpler than they are; can pull from many sources, see the importance of many factors.

UNSKILLED

Prefers to keep things simple; may not have good conceptual buckets to put disparate data in; may be thrown by problems or situations that don't fit.

ITEMS

- ☐ 2. Is intellectually quick; picks up on things in a hurry.
- ☐ 29. Can project consequences and how things are connected.
- ☐ 56. Is comfortable with complexity.

LEADERSHIP ARCHITECT® COMPETENCIES MOST ASSOCIATED WITH THIS DIMENSION

Strong

- ☐ 2. *Dealing with* Ambiguity
- ☐ 14. Creativity
- ☐ 32. Learning on the Fly
- ☐ 51. Problem Solving

Moderate

- ☐ 30. Intellectual Horsepower
- ☐ 46. Perspective
- ☐ 52. Process Management
- ☐ 58. Strategic Agility
- ☐ 61. Technical Learning

Light

☐ 50. Priority Setting

SOME CAUSES

☐ Doesn't think beyond one's own work/tasks

☐ Gets frustrated when he/she isn't in the know

☐ Gets stressed and overwhelmed easily

☐ Impatient

☐ Low tolerance for ambiguity and uncertainty

☐ Narrow background

☐ Not comfortable with not knowing, not answering; can't say I don't know

☐ Not strategic; doesn't anticipate outcomes

☐ Overly results driven

☐ Oversimplifies

☐ Single-tracked

☐ Slow to catch on

☐ Too specialized

THE MAP

Complexity is a part of life. And it is probably increasing, especially in the area of life and work technologies. People who offer truly simple explanations and solutions to complex problems will have had to understand its complexity first. Globalization and speed are adding to the complexity. While trying to get everything to be simple is a worthy goal, it is probably not reflective of truth.

SOME REMEDIES

☐ 1. Coming to quick, simple solutions is the bane of many a problem solver. Practice adding complexity and resisting the urge to just decide. To do this, ask how many elements or factors does this problem have? What is related to it? What is not related to it?

☐ 2. Put all like elements into conceptual buckets. For example, everything to do with costing in one bucket, everything having to do with people in another. Analyze how the buckets can work together and how they work against each other. Create processes for each bucket and processes for the buckets as a whole.

☐ 3. Resist saying you know what causes a problem. Most issues worth considering are multi-causal. Ask why or how this could be a cause to better understand the nature of the beast. What would you accept as evidence that your problem definition is correct? What consequences would occur? What wouldn't occur? What are you prepared to do if your definition is incorrect?

☐ 4. If you make decisions too quickly, work to better understand your patience triggers. Is time pressure one of them? Do you make quick decisions just to check something off your list or get someone out of your hair? Analyze the factors that cause you to avoid taking the time to consider complexity, and discipline yourself to spend half your problem solving time defining the problem and thinking about all of its elements. Even if that's only ten minutes, use five to look more thoroughly.

☐ 5. Since studies show that defining a problem and taking action happen almost simultaneously, you may as well load more effort on the front end. That's your best chance of a breakthrough solution. Discipline yourself to go for the second and third solution—the "what else could we do" question. Studies show the second or third solutions are often superior.

☐ 6. Ask more questions. Studies have shown that about 50 percent of discussions involve answers; only 7 percent involve probing questions. Why does that work? Why might my solution not work this time? How would I know if it did or didn't? What's least likely? What's missing from the problem?

☐ 7. **(Workaround)** If you have people working for you, push back on them continually coming to you for solutions. If you create an environment that encourages others to probe problems more deeply, you may be able to compensate for your own shortcomings.

☐ 8. **(Workaround)** Ask a subject-matter expert in the area of the problem to help you define the parameters of the problem. If your experiences are narrow or unrelated to the problem, you may need to learn to ask for help to get to the right solution.

☐ 9. **(Workaround)** Find other examples of how others have approached this or similar problems.

☐ 10. **(Workaround)** Hire one or two people who are especially good at this and delegate the task to them. Ask for regular updates so that you learn and understand the techniques and processes they use to solve complex problems.

MORE HELP?

See *FYI For Your Improvement*™. We have coded each item to about 10 tips from the *FYI* book. To use this resource, the codes below refer to the chapter and then the tip number from the *FYI* book. For example, in item 2 below, 1-5 refers to Chapter 1—Action Oriented, tip 5. If you don't have a copy of *FYI*, it is available through Lominger at 952-345-3610 or www.lominger.com

2. Is intellectually quick; picks up on things in a hurry.
1-5; 14-4; 16-4; 30-4; 32-1,2,3,5,9; 58-4

29. Can project consequences and how things are connected.
17-2,3; 32-1,2,3; 46-1,2; 58-3,4,6

56. Is comfortable with complexity.
2-1,2,5; 14-4; 17-3; 32-2,3; 58-4; 101-6; 118-8

JOBS THAT WOULD ADD SKILLS IN THIS DIMENSION

☐ Scope (very broad) Assignments—managing a high variety of activities.

☐ Heavy Strategic Demands—charting new ground for products/services.

☐ Fix-its/Turnarounds—requiring lots of decisions on incomplete data in a short time frame.

PART-TIME ASSIGNMENTS THAT WOULD ADD SKILLS IN THIS DIMENSION

☐ Relaunch an existing product/service that's not doing well.

☐ Work with a highly diverse team to accomplish a difficult task.

☐ Manage a group where they are more expert in the technology than you are.

☐ Work on a project that involves travel, benchmarking, and exploration of issues and topics you have never studied before.

☐ Work on a multifunctional team trying to solve an issue that crosses boundaries in the organization.

☐ Work on a team that has to integrate diverse systems (move from using five computer platforms into one), processes (moving from ISO, TQM, and Six Sigma into only one of the three), or procedures (five competency models into one) across decentralized and/or dispersed units.

☐ Do a competitive analysis of your organization's product or services and your position in the marketplace and present it to senior decision makers.

SUGGESTED READINGS

De Bono, Edward. *Six thinking hats*. Boston: Little, Brown, 1985.

Drucker, P. *Management challenges for the 21st century*. New York: HarperBusiness, 1999.

Dudik, E. *Strategic renaissance*. New York: AMACOM, 2000.

Epstein, Seymour, Ph.D. with Archie Brodsky. *You're smarter than you think—How to develop your practical intelligence for success in living*. New York: Simon & Schuster, 1993.

Glassman, Peter J. *J.S. Mill: The evolution of a genius*. Gainesville: University of Florida Press, 1985.

Hale, Guy. *The leader's edge—Mastering the five skills of break-through thinking*. Burr Ridge, IL: Irwin Professional Publishing, 1996.

Hamel, Gary. *Leading the revolution*. Watertown, MA: Harvard Business School Press, 2000.

Hamel, Gary and C.K. Prahalad. *Competing for the future*. Boston, MA: Harvard Business School Press, 1994.

Kennedy, Paul M. *The rise and fall of the great powers: Economic change and military conflict from 1500 to 2000*. New York: Random House, 1987.

Nadler, Gerald, Ph.D. and Shozo Hibino, Ph.D. *Breakthrough thinking—The seven principles of creative problem solving*. Rocklin, CA: Prima Publishing, 1998.

Porter, Michael E. *On competition*. Boston: Harvard Business School Press, 1998.

Prahalad, C.K. and Venkat Ramaswamy. *The future of competition: Co-creating unique value with customers*. Harvard Business School Press, February 18, 2004.

2

DIMENSION 3
CONNECTOR

3

SKILLED

Intellectually rigorous; looks deeply at many sources, hunts for parallels, contrasts, unique combinations. Isn't afraid to go off on an intellectual tangent and take time to think through something.

UNSKILLED

May be intellectually lazy, think he/she already knows the answer, or even be too quick to act; may be ahistorical, doesn't hunt for fresh views or solutions. If action-oriented, this may mask dislike or disdain for detailed problem searches or looking for seemingly obscure parallels.

ITEMS

- ☐ 3. Can point out and find parallels, perspectives, contrasts, contexts, connections or combinations.
- ☐ 30. Uses multiple sources to get data and answers.
- ☐ 57. Is able to connect things others don't see as related.

LEADERSHIP ARCHITECT® COMPETENCIES MOST ASSOCIATED WITH THIS DIMENSION

Strong

- ☐ 2. *Dealing with* Ambiguity
- ☐ 14. Creativity
- ☐ 32. Learning on the Fly
- ☐ 46. Perspective
- ☐ 51. Problem Solving
- ☐ 52. Process Management

Moderate

☐ 30. Intellectual Horsepower

☐ 58. Strategic Agility

Light

☐ 17. Decision Quality

SOME CAUSES

☐ Arrogant, know it all

☐ Cautious

☐ Impatient

☐ Intellectually lazy; doesn't apply self

☐ Intimidated by other sources

☐ Limited ways to think

☐ Low tolerance of ambiguity and uncertainty

☐ Narrow or disadvantaged background

☐ Not curious

☐ Only skims the surface

☐ Rejects speculation

☐ Relies too much on self

☐ Restrained

☐ Single-tracked

☐ Sticks with the proven

☐ Too specialized

☐ Won't admit when he/she doesn't know something

16

THE MAP

Creativity is defined as connecting two knowns that were previously unconnected. If you restrict yourself to the connections you currently make, you'll only come up with breakthrough ideas by sheer chance. Things repeatedly repeat in life. Similar things happen in parallel areas of life. Almost nothing is truly new. Almost everything has already happened. You can increase your chances of success by learning from the lessons of history and making connections across usually isolated areas.

SOME REMEDIES

☐ 1. Make your mind a bit sillier. You don't have to tell anyone what you're doing. Ask what song is this problem like? Find an analogy to your problem in nature, in children's toys, in anything that has a physical structure. Silly parallels can help you create the rules of thumb for the serious ones.

☐ 2. Ask what's the least likely reason for something to happen, then connect it to the most likely. Build a scale or measure of least to most likelihoods to gauge the scenario.

☐ 3. Look for anomalies, unusual facts that don't quite fit in. Why did sales go down when they should have gone up? It could be random, but maybe not. The unusual facts can help you to determine hidden causes and effects, measures, and other helpful pieces of data.

☐ 4. Look for what was always present in a success but was never present in a failure. Or, look for what was always present in a failure but never present in a success. What are the critical contrasts? How can they be applied to other things you encounter?

☐ 5. Hunt for parallels in other organizations and in remote areas totally outside your field. By this we don't mean best practices, which come and go. Find a parallel situation to the underlying issue—for example, who has to do things really fast (Domino's,

17

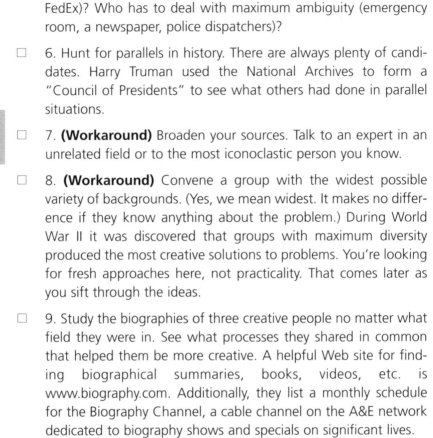

FedEx)? Who has to deal with maximum ambiguity (emergency room, a newspaper, police dispatchers)?

☐ 6. Hunt for parallels in history. There are always plenty of candidates. Harry Truman used the National Archives to form a "Council of Presidents" to see what others had done in parallel situations.

☐ 7. **(Workaround)** Broaden your sources. Talk to an expert in an unrelated field or to the most iconoclastic person you know.

☐ 8. **(Workaround)** Convene a group with the widest possible variety of backgrounds. (Yes, we mean widest. It makes no difference if they know anything about the problem.) During World War II it was discovered that groups with maximum diversity produced the most creative solutions to problems. You're looking for fresh approaches here, not practicality. That comes later as you sift through the ideas.

☐ 9. Study the biographies of three creative people no matter what field they were in. See what processes they shared in common that helped them be more creative. A helpful Web site for finding biographical summaries, books, videos, etc. is www.biography.com. Additionally, they list a monthly schedule for the Biography Channel, a cable channel on the A&E network dedicated to biography shows and specials on significant lives.

☐ 10. **(Workaround)** Use an internal or external consultant or subject-matter experts to help move beyond the obvious and beyond what most others would come up with. Ask questions of the consultants to learn from their problem solving techniques. How do they collect data? How do they analyze it?

MORE HELP?

See *FYI For Your Improvement*™. We have coded each item to about 10 tips from the *FYI* book. To use this resource, the codes below refer to the chapter and then the tip number from the *FYI* book. For example, in item 3 below, 17-3,5 refers to Chapter 17—Decision

Quality, tips 3 and 5. If you don't have a copy of *FYI*, it is available through Lominger at 952-345-3610 or www.lominger.com

3. Can point out and find parallels, perspectives, contrasts, contexts, connections or combinations.
   17-3,5; 30-2,6; 32-1,2,3,10; 41-7; 101-3

30. Uses multiple sources to get data and answers.
   14-2,3,4; 17-3; 30-2; 32-5,7; 33-3; 41-7; 101-3

57. Is able to connect things others don't see as related.
   14-1,2,3,4; 32-1,2,3; 46-4,5,6

JOBS THAT WOULD ADD SKILLS IN THIS DIMENSION

☐ Scope (very broad) Assignments—managing a high variety of activities.

☐ Heavy Strategic Demands—charting new ground for products/services that will require collecting and analyzing lots of data.

☐ Start-ups—requiring doing first-time things drawing from diverse sources.

☐ Fix-its/Turnarounds—requiring lots of decisions on incomplete data in a short time frame.

☐ Out of Home Country Assignments—where you have to make the connection between your background and this new setting.

PART-TIME ASSIGNMENTS THAT WOULD ADD SKILLS IN THIS DIMENSION

☐ Work with a highly diverse team to accomplish a difficult task.

☐ Relaunch an existing product/service that's not doing well.

☐ Take on a tough and undoable project where others have failed.

☐ Work on a team fixing something that has failed.

☐ Work on a team managing a significant business crisis (workplace violence, Tylenol scare, Bhopal).

☐ Work on a multifunctional team trying to solve an issue that crosses boundaries in the organization.

SUGGESTED READINGS

De Bono, Edward. *Six thinking hats*. Boston: Little, Brown, 1985.

Drucker, P. *Management challenges for the 21st century*. New York: HarperBusiness, 1999.

Epstein, Seymour, Ph.D. with Archie Brodsky. *You're smarter than you think—How to develop your practical intelligence for success in living*. New York: Simon & Schuster, 1993.

Glassman, Peter J. *J.S. Mill: The evolution of a genius*. Gainesville: University of Florida Press, 1985.

Hale, Guy. *The leader's edge—Mastering the five skills of breakthrough thinking*. Burr Ridge, IL: Irwin Professional Publishing, 1996.

Hamel, Gary. *Leading the revolution*. Watertown, MA: Harvard Business School Press, 2000.

Hamel, Gary and C.K. Prahalad. *Competing for the future*. Boston, MA: Harvard Business School Press, 1994.

Keen, Peter G.W. *The process edge—Creating value where it counts*. Boston: Harvard Business School Press, 1998.

Kennedy, Paul M. *The rise and fall of the great powers: Economic change and military conflict from 1500 to 2000*. New York, NY: Random House, 1987.

Nadler, Gerald, Ph.D. and Shozo Hibino, Ph.D. *Breakthrough thinking—The seven principles of creative problem solving*. Rocklin, CA: Prima Publishing, 1998.

Prahalad, C.K. and Venkat Ramaswamy. *The future of competition: Co-creating unique value with customers*. Harvard Business School Press, February 18, 2004.

The Systems Thinker®. Waltham, MA: Pegasus Communications, Inc., 781-398-9700.

DIMENSION 4
CRITICAL THINKER

SKILLED
Takes the time to look at and question conventional wisdom; doesn't accept much as a given; looks beyond.

UNSKILLED
May have trouble with ideas that don't fit, violate what's been done in the past, or are uncomfortable. May simply like the predictability of known solutions.

ITEMS
- ☐ 4. Faces paradox; can look at ideas or solutions that violate common sense and yet might still be true.
- ☐ 31. Usually takes time to critically examine conventional wisdom and givens before moving on.
- ☐ 58. Is a good questioner of self and others.

LEADERSHIP ARCHITECT® COMPETENCIES MOST ASSOCIATED WITH THIS DIMENSION

Strong
- ☐ 41. Patience
- ☐ 46. Perspective
- ☐ 51. Problem Solving

Moderate
- ☐ 2. *Dealing with* Ambiguity
- ☐ 14. Creativity
- ☐ 33. Listening
- ☐ 40. *Dealing with* Paradox

Light

- ☐ 32. Learning on the Fly
- ☐ 52. Process Management
- ☐ 62. Time Management

SOME CAUSES

- ☐ Active biases
- ☐ Conventional
- ☐ Disinterest
- ☐ Doesn't read people
- ☐ Doesn't read situations
- ☐ Fear of being different
- ☐ Impatient
- ☐ Low tolerance of ambiguity
- ☐ Narrow background
- ☐ Not challenged
- ☐ Not curious
- ☐ Rigid
- ☐ Strong beliefs
- ☐ Too trusting of others

THE MAP

Do you pretty much go with your history of what has worked for you and others? Do you like predictability? Uncomfortable with odd notions? Uncomfortable with going against group opinion or prefer to decide alone? If so, you're restricting your decision making, problem solving flexibility. All issues and problems have some portion of uniqueness to them. Almost nothing is the same the second or third time. Question what is. Don't take things for granted.

SOME REMEDIES

☐ 1. Think out loud. Figure out what you really think by describing the issue or problem to another person. Find a solid sounding board or go to the most irreverent person you know. Look for people who will challenge your thinking and have the courage to push back.

☐ 2. Practice the rules of brainstorming in group settings. Lots of ideas, no evaluation. Encourage any form of participation, don't restrict idea flow.

☐ 3. Ask more questions. Studies have shown that about 50 percent of discussions involve answers; only 7 percent involve probing questions. Why does that work? Why might my solution not work this time? How would I know if it did or didn't? What's least likely? What's missing from the problem?

☐ 4. Write down your best solution then throw it out. Come up with a second and a third. Now decide which one is best. Research has shown that most of the time the best answer isn't the first one you come up with.

☐ 5. Think small. Make small decisions, get feedback, correct errors, get more data, move forward a bit more. Up your comfort with ambiguity by dealing with it in bite-size chunks.

☐ 6. Define the problem, don't put it in a familiar box so you can feel comfortable. What is it and what isn't it? How many causes can you think of? Are you stating things as facts that are really your opinion? Are you generalizing from an example or two? Use patterns and themes to define problems.

☐ 7. Go against the grain. Be able to state in a few sentences why a lone view you hold might be correct. Build a case around business or system issues; don't let it get personal. Be able to state opposing views as well as detractors can.

☐ 8. **(Workaround)** Find external or internal people who are by nature critical thinkers who have no stake in the issue or the answers. Let them work on the problem before you do. Have them prepare as many alternatives that they can for you to choose from.

☐ 9. **(Workaround)** Look to how others have approached and solved this issue or problem before you. Or have some staff support people research the issue or problem and urge them to find as many different and unique solutions as they can.

☐ 10. Evaluate your solutions by doing downstream "what if" analyses. How does this impact other issues/people/customers/ suppliers, etc.? Many times there are unanticipated consequences to otherwise good-sounding solutions. You might be able to find and select better solutions by visualizing what would follow if your proposed solutions were implemented.

MORE HELP?

See *FYI For Your Improvement™*. We have coded each item to about 10 tips from the *FYI* book. To use this resource, the codes below refer to the chapter and then the tip number from the *FYI* book. For example, in item 4 below, 14-1,2,3,4,5 refers to Chapter 14— Creativity, tips 1–5. If you don't have a copy of *FYI*, it is available through Lominger at 952-345-3610 or www.lominger.com

4. Faces paradox; can look at ideas or solutions that violate common sense and yet might still be true.
14-1,2,3,4,5; 51-3,4; 101-2,3; 118-8

31. Usually takes time to critically examine conventional wisdom and givens before moving on.
14-2; 51-1,2,3,4,5,8; 58-3; 101-2,6

58. Is a good questioner of self and others.
31-2; 32-1,2,3; 33-1,2,3,4,8; 51-1

JOBS THAT WOULD ADD SKILLS IN THIS DIMENSION

☐ Scope (very broad) Assignments—managing a high variety of activities.

☐ Heavy Strategic Demands—charting new ground for products/services.

☐ Out of Home Country Assignments—where you have to think through problems from a novel position and for this new setting.

☐ Start-ups—requiring doing first-time things drawing from diverse sources.

PART-TIME ASSIGNMENTS THAT WOULD ADD SKILLS IN THIS DIMENSION

☐ Work with a highly diverse team to accomplish a difficult task.

☐ Relaunch an existing product/service that's not doing well.

☐ Take on a tough and undoable project where others have failed.

☐ Work on a team fixing something that has failed.

☐ Work on a team managing a significant business crisis (work-place violence, Tylenol scare, Bhopal).

☐ Prepare and present a proposal of some consequence to top management (and anticipate the questions that senior leaders will pose).

☐ Work on a team that has to integrate diverse systems (move from using five computer platforms into one), processes (moving from ISO, TQM, and Six Sigma into only one of the three), or procedures (five competency models into one) across decentralized and/or dispersed units.

SUGGESTED READINGS

De Bono, Edward. *Six thinking hats*. Boston: Little, Brown, 1985.

Epstein, Seymour, Ph.D. with Archie Brodsky. *You're smarter than you think—How to develop your practical intelligence for success in living*. New York: Simon & Schuster, 1993.

Glassman, Peter J. *J.S. Mill: The evolution of a genius*. Gainesville: University of Florida Press, 1985.

Hale, Guy. *The leader's edge—Mastering the five skills of breakthrough thinking*. Burr Ridge, IL: Irwin Professional Publishing, 1996.

Handy, Charles. *The age of paradox*. Boston: Harvard Business School Press, 1994.

Keen, Peter G.W. *The process edge—Creating value where it counts*. Boston: Harvard Business School Press, 1998.

Kennedy, Paul M. *The rise and fall of the great powers: Economic change and military conflict from 1500 to 2000*. New York, NY: Random House, 1987.

Nadler, Gerald, Ph.D. and Shozo Hibino, Ph.D. *Breakthrough thinking—The seven principles of creative problem solving*. Rocklin, CA: Prima Publishing, 1998.

Nichols, Michael P. *The lost art of listening*. New York: The Guilford Press, 1995.

The Systems Thinker®. Waltham, MA: Pegasus Communications, Inc., 781-398-9700.

Dimension 5
Easy Shifter

SKILLED

Comfortable when things are up in the air; shifts gears easily.

UNSKILLED

May be uncomfortable with ambiguity, or likes to stick to one action/ solution rather than change courses.

ITEMS

- ☐ 5. Easily shifts gears from one action/solution to another.
- ☐ 32. Functions as effectively under conditions of ambiguity as when things are more certain.
- ☐ 59. Is comfortable when things are ambiguous, uncertain, or up in the air.

LEADERSHIP ARCHITECT® COMPETENCIES MOST ASSOCIATED WITH THIS DIMENSION

Strong

- ☐ 2. *Dealing with* Ambiguity
- ☐ 32. Learning on the Fly
- ☐ 40. *Dealing with* Paradox

Moderate

- ☐ 11. Composure
- ☐ 39. Organizing
- ☐ 50. Priority Setting
- ☐ 51. Problem Solving

Light

☐   1. Action Oriented

☐ 16. *Timely* Decision Making

☐ 46. Perspective

☐ 57. Standing Alone

SOME CAUSES

☐ Can't multi-task

☐ Cautious

☐ Dislikes change

☐ Gets stressed or overwhelmed easily

☐ High need to close

☐ High need to finish

☐ Impatient

☐ Lack of composure

☐ Low frustration tolerance

☐ Low tolerance of ambiguity

☐ Needs to be sure and certain

☐ Perfectionist

☐ Prefers structure and control

THE MAP

Dealing with change is synonymous with dealing with ambiguity. Some studies estimate that 90 percent of what managers deal with is at least somewhat ambiguous. The world is getting less and less predictable. Those more tolerant of ambiguity and uncertainty will do better. The half-life of solutions, styles, or habits is getting shorter. Nothing lasts very long. Change is what's happening. Change is uncertain.

28

SOME REMEDIES

☐ 1. Do quick experiments. Studies show that 80 percent of innovations occur in the wrong place or are created by the wrong people working on something else. Test something out, study the results, learn, do it a little better the next time.

☐ 2. All of us have to shift behavior each day. We act differently when things run well and when they don't. We act differently with different people. Study the transitions you make each day and write down which ones give you the most trouble and why. Are they more people related, process related, schedule related, etc.?

☐ 3. Devise strategies to deal with uncomfortable situations. If you get sharp under pressure, use some humor to counter this tendency. If you're too tough on others, ask yourself how you'd like to be treated in this situation.

☐ 4. Use mental rehearsal for tough situations. Learn to recognize the clues that you're about to fall back on old behavior and be ready with a fresh strategy that you have decided in advance. If you know, for example, that a solution isn't working and you're likely to be questioned about it, be ready to engage others and get the benefit of their thinking.

☐ 5. Don't try to get it totally right the first time. If a situation is ambiguous, be incremental. Make some small decisions, get instant feedback, treat mistakes and failures as ways to learn. Focus on your third or fourth try, not the first.

☐ 6. Have an answer or solution to most things? Trying to wipe out uncertainty by plucking an answer from your hat? If you jump to conclusions or dismiss others' ideas, this is probably getting you into trouble. Use gentler words, ask questions, let others talk without interruption, pause to see what others have to say.

☐ 7. **(Workaround)** Pattern your response to uncertainty and ambiguity after someone around you that doesn't seem to be bothered when things are up in the air. Worry when they do; relax when they are relaxed about what is going on.

5

☐ 8. Study the lives of people who have done well under conditions of ambiguity and uncertainty. Read their biographies or autobiographies. What did they do under time of high chaos? A helpful Web site for finding biographical summaries, books, videos, etc. is www.biography.com. Additionally, they list a monthly schedule for the Biography Channel, a cable channel on the A&E network dedicated to biography shows and specials on significant lives.

☐ 9. Trim the uncertainty. Break it down into pieces. Nothing is really ever totally uncertain. Solve the little things and get them out of the way. Do something. Generally little actions will trim the size of the uncertainty until is gets small enough to comfortably tackle.

☐ 10. Work on leaving things undone and unfinished. Move on to something else. Take a break. Clear your head. The brain has the capacity to continue to work on the problem while you are doing something else. Many times, the solutions will occur to you when you are doing something completely different or even when you are sleeping!

MORE HELP?

See *FYI For Your Improvement*™. We have coded each item to about 10 tips from the *FYI* book. To use this resource, the codes below refer to the chapter and then the tip number from the *FYI* book. For example, in item 5 below, 32-1,8,9 refers to Chapter 32—Learning on the Fly, tips 1,8,9. If you don't have a copy of *FYI*, it is available through Lominger at 952-345-3610 or www.lominger.com

5. Easily shifts gears from one action/solution to another.
   32-1,8,9; 40-1,2,3,5,9,10; 118-8

32. Functions as effectively under conditions of ambiguity as when things are more certain.
    2-2,3,7,9; 16-4; 58-4; 101-1,2,3,6

59. Is comfortable when things are ambiguous, uncertain, or up in the air.
    2-2,3,7,9; 16-4; 58-4; 101-1,2,3,6

JOBS THAT WOULD ADD SKILLS IN THIS DIMENSION

☐ Chair of Projects/Taskforces—where the role is different than a straight manager, with diversity in the group, with tight deadlines, and multiple constituencies.

☐ Scope (very broad) Assignments—managing a high variety of activities.

☐ Start-ups—requiring doing a lot of first-time things, shifting from role to role in a very short period of time.

☐ Fix-its/Turnarounds—requiring lots of different decisions and actions in a short period of time.

PART-TIME ASSIGNMENTS THAT WOULD ADD SKILLS IN THIS DIMENSION

☐ Work on a team fixing something that has failed.

☐ Take on a tough and undoable project where others have failed.

☐ Work with a highly diverse team to accomplish a difficult task.

☐ Plan a new site for a building or installation (plant, field office, headquarters, etc.).

☐ Help shut down a plant, region, country product line, service, operation that has been around a reasonable amount of time.

☐ Work on a multifunctional team trying to solve an issue that crosses boundaries in the organization.

☐ Relaunch an existing product/service that's not doing well.

☐ Work on a team managing a significant business crisis (workplace violence, Tylenol scare, Bhopal).

☐ Manage a group where they are more expert in the technology than you are.

SUGGESTED READINGS

De Bono, Edward. *Six thinking hats*. Boston: Little, Brown, 1985.

Epstein, Seymour, Ph.D. with Archie Brodsky. *You're smarter than you think—How to develop your practical intelligence for success in living*. New York: Simon & Schuster, 1993.

Glassman, Peter J. *J.S. Mill: The evolution of a genius*. Gainesville: University of Florida Press, 1985.

Hale, Guy. *The leader's edge—Mastering the five skills of breakthrough thinking*. Burr Ridge, IL: Irwin Professional Publishing, 1996.

Handy, Charles. *The age of unreason*. Boston: Harvard Business School Press, 1989.

Handy, Charles. *The age of paradox*. Boston: Harvard Business School Press, 1994.

Keen, Peter G.W. *The process edge—Creating value where it counts*. Boston: Harvard Business School Press, 1998.

Kennedy, Paul M. *The rise and fall of the great powers: Economic change and military conflict from 1500 to 2000*. New York, NY: Random House, 1987.

Loehr, James E. *Stress for success*. New York: Times Business, 1997.

Nadler, Gerald, Ph.D. and Shozo Hibino, Ph.D. *Breakthrough thinking—The seven principles of creative problem solving*. Rocklin, CA: Prima Publishing, 1998.

Nichols, Michael P. *The lost art of listening*. New York: The Guilford Press, 1995.

The Systems Thinker®. Waltham, MA: Pegasus Communications, Inc., 781-398-9700.

DIMENSION 6
ESSENCE

SKILLED

Looks for root causes; interested in why; good at separating the more from the less important.

UNSKILLED

May be too caught up in single events or problems and fail to see the pattern; may focus too narrowly on solutions based on present conditions; may view most things as about equally important and not differentiate well among different activities. At the extreme, could be an action junkie.

ITEMS

- ☐ 6. Prefers to get to the root causes of things.
- ☐ 33. Likes finding the essence of why things work and don't work.
- ☐ 60. Looks for the why and how of events and experiences more than the what; searches for meaning.

LEADERSHIP ARCHITECT® COMPETENCIES MOST ASSOCIATED WITH THIS DIMENSION

Strong

- ☐ 2. *Dealing with* Ambiguity
- ☐ 46. Perspective
- ☐ 51. Problem Solving

Moderate

- ☐ 32. Learning on the Fly
- ☐ 50. Priority Setting
- ☐ 52. Process Management

Light

- ☐ 17. Decision Quality
- ☐ 41. Patience
- ☐ 43. Perseverance

SOME CAUSES

- ☐ Complexifier
- ☐ Doesn't get to the point
- ☐ Doesn't go deep
- ☐ High need for speed
- ☐ High need to close
- ☐ Impatient
- ☐ Narrow background
- ☐ Not challenged
- ☐ Not curious
- ☐ Not strategic
- ☐ Satisfied with a temporary fix

THE MAP

Looking to patterns of how and why something works is what produces a robust solution. Simply looking at what has worked can be misleading as it may have only worked in certain conditions that no longer apply. To solve problems better, we need to understand patterns and causes. If you can get to the essence, then you can propose and implement the simplest and most elegant solution.

SOME REMEDIES

- ☐ 1. See how many causes for things you can come up with and how many categories you can put them in. Then ask what they have in common and how they are different.

☐ 2. Check for common errors in thinking. Do you state as facts things that are really opinions or assumptions? Do your feelings or emotions get in the way of issues? Do you attribute cause and effect to relationships when you don't know if one causes the other? Do you generalize from a single example? Do you treat all aspects of a problem as if they are equally important?

☐ 3. Study successes and ask what they have in common. If you can find three times that something worked, ask why it worked despite differences in the situations. Also ask what was present in a failure that was never present in a success. Then you are on the way to finding principles that may repeat.

☐ 4. Take time to think. Add a few minutes to your thinking time, go through a mental checklist without jumping at the first option. Since defining a problem and taking action tend to occur simultaneously, spend more time up front.

☐ 5. Locate the essence of a problem by figuring out its key elements. Experts usually figure out problems by locating the deep underlying principles and working forward from there. The less adept focus on desired outcomes/solutions and either work backward or focus on surface facts.

☐ 6. Hunt for parallels in other organizations and in remote areas totally outside your field. By this we don't mean best practices, which come and go. Find a parallel situation to the underlying issue—for example, who has to do things really fast (Domino's, FedEx)? Who has to deal with maximum ambiguity (emergency room, a newspaper, police dispatchers)?

☐ 7. Throughout the history of thought, the proposition has been put forward that the solution with the least number of elements or factors is probably the most correct one. See how few reasons you can create that explain the issue.

☐ 8. There is a progression of getting to the essence of a problem or issue. Generally, problem solving starts with simplistic solutions to complex problems. First, everyone proposes a solution even before there is a clear definition of the problem. The second stage is complexification. Someone always blows the issue out into its ultimate completeness with boxes and arrows. Many times it is correct, but very involved and complex. The third stage is parsimony. Someone takes all of the complexity and trims it down into the understandable. Some accuracy is lost. The last stage is simplicity or essence. Someone trims to the ultimate foundation rock basis of the issue with an elegant and simple explanation or solution. One problem is that the simplistic and the simple look alike, although one is incorrect and the other accurate. The trick is to take the problem though the four stages. That takes patience. You can't get to the essence until you understand the complex.

☐ 9. **(Workaround)** Engage internal or external essence detectors, people who enjoy and are good at getting to the very bottom of things. Give them everything you know and let them work at it for a while and report back. Ask them to walk you through their process for reaching the conclusions they've drawn.

☐ 10. **(Workaround)** In a sense, there are no new problems. Almost all problems have a history. It may be a new problem to you but probably not to the world. Look to history. See what people have done in the past. What did everyone decide, well after the fact, were the real causes and the real solutions?

MORE HELP?

See *FYI For Your Improvement*™. We have coded each item to about 10 tips from the *FYI* book. To use this resource, the codes below refer to the chapter and then the tip number from the *FYI* book. For example, in item 6 below, 17-3 refers to Chapter 17—Decision Quality, tip 3. If you don't have a copy of *FYI*, it is available through Lominger at 952-345-3610 or www.lominger.com

6. Prefers to get to the root causes of things.
   17-3; 30-2,6; 32-1,2,3,10; 41-7; 51-1; 101-3

33. Likes finding the essence of why things work and don't work.
   17-3; 30-2,6; 32-1,2,3,10; 41-7; 51-1; 101-3

60. Looks for the why and how of events and experiences more than the what; searches for meaning.
17-3; 30-2,6; 32-1,2,3,10; 41-7; 51-1; 101-3

JOBS THAT WOULD ADD SKILLS IN THIS DIMENSION

☐ Influencing Without Authority—finding solutions to tough problems with insufficient direct power to make anything happen. The politics of the job are usually sensitive and opposition is common.

☐ Fix-its/Turnarounds—requiring identifying the essential elements that cause the failure and the essential elements that will fix it.

☐ Heavy Strategic Demands—finding the essence of a new direction.

☐ Out of Home Country Assignments—where you have to identify the essential; things to do and the essential differences from what you have known and done in the past.

PART-TIME ASSIGNMENTS THAT WOULD ADD SKILLS IN THIS DIMENSION

☐ Work with a highly diverse team to accomplish a difficult task.

☐ Work on a team fixing something that has failed.

☐ Take on a tough and undoable project where others have failed.

☐ Work on a team that has to integrate diverse systems (move from using five computer platforms into one), processes (moving from ISO, TQM, and Six Sigma into only one of the three), or procedures (five competency models into one) across decentralized and/or dispersed units where you have to boil things down to their essence.

☐ Relaunch an existing product/service that's not doing well.

☐ Work on a multifunctional team trying to solve an issue that crosses boundaries in the organization.

☐ Plan a new site for a building or installation (plant, field office, headquarters, etc.).

- ☐ Handle a tough negotiation with an external or internal customer, a union, a key vendor, or a dissatisfied customer.

- ☐ Work on a team managing a significant business crisis (workplace violence, Tylenol scare, Bhopal).

- ☐ Work on a team deciding who to lay off and what to shut down to trim costs.

SUGGESTED READINGS

De Bono, Edward. *Six thinking hats*. Boston: Little, Brown, 1985.

Epstein, Seymour, Ph.D. with Archie Brodsky. *You're smarter than you think—How to develop your practical intelligence for success in living*. New York: Simon & Schuster, 1993.

Glassman, Peter J. *J.S. Mill: The evolution of a genius*. Gainesville: University of Florida Press, 1985.

Hale, Guy. *The leader's edge—Mastering the five skills of breakthrough thinking*. Burr Ridge, IL: Irwin Professional Publishing, 1996.

Handy, Charles. *The age of paradox*. Boston: Harvard Business School Press, 1994.

Keen, Peter G.W. *The process edge—Creating value where it counts*. Boston: Harvard Business School Press, 1998.

Nadler, Gerald, Ph.D. and Shozo Hibino, Ph.D. *Breakthrough thinking—The seven principles of creative problem solving*. Rocklin, CA: Prima Publishing, 1998.

Nichols, Michael P. *The lost art of listening*. New York: The Guilford Press, 1995.

The Systems Thinker®. Waltham, MA: Pegasus Communications, Inc., 781-398-9700.

DIMENSION 7
INQUISITIVE

SKILLED
Searches for the new; curious, likes to have many things going at once.

UNSKILLED
Likes the familiar; may prefer to work on one thing at a time, go to comfortable sources, or be with comfortable people who won't challenge present conceptions.

ITEMS
- ☐ 7. Is on the hunt for something new; seems to need fresh challenges.
- ☐ 34. Is more fascinated, amused, or intrigued with tough problems and challenges than stressed, troubled, or strained.
- ☐ 61. Is a curious person; is intellectually adventuresome.

LEADERSHIP ARCHITECT® COMPETENCIES MOST ASSOCIATED WITH THIS DIMENSION

Strong
- ☐ 2. *Dealing with* Ambiguity
- ☐ 14. Creativity

Moderate
- ☐ 32. Learning on the Fly
- ☐ 46. Perspective
- ☐ 51. Problem Solving

Light

- ☐ 1. Action Oriented
- ☐ 28. Innovation Management
- ☐ 61. Technical Learning

SOME CAUSES

- ☐ Can't get out of the box
- ☐ Can't shift gears quickly
- ☐ Comfortable with what is
- ☐ Conventional
- ☐ Fear of uncertainty
- ☐ Gets frustrated easily
- ☐ Has a need to finish things before moving on
- ☐ Impatient
- ☐ Intimidated by things and people who are different
- ☐ Narrow background
- ☐ Not challenged
- ☐ Not curious
- ☐ Not wanting to be the only one out front
- ☐ Perfectionist

THE MAP

Most of us fall into habitual ways of thinking and acting, and this in turn leads to diminishing our creativity and problem solving skills. Learning about something new increases the chance of making novel connections. The curious always find the treasure.

SOME REMEDIES

☐ 1. Explore new ground. Take a course in an area you know nothing about. Take a course in an area only sort of related to what you do. Go to restaurants you know nothing about. Vacation at places you've never been before. Talk to more strangers in line at the grocery store and on airplanes. Go to ethnic festivals. Read the book series called *How Things Work*. Watch the Discovery Channel's series called *Connections*.

☐ 2. Take more risks. Research indicates that more successful people have made more mistakes than the less successful. You can't learn anything if you're not trying anything new. Start small and experiment a bit. Go for small wins so you can recover quickly if you miss, and more important, learn from the results. Start with the easiest challenge, then work up to the tougher ones.

☐ 3. Are you bored or uncommitted? Seen it all, done the same tasks again and again. Start with a list of what you like and don't like to do. Do at least a couple of liked activities each day, but follow a basic rule of psychology—least preferred activities first. Reward yourself with the liked activities. Volunteer for task forces and projects that you would enjoy to modify your job. Don't focus on the activities you dislike—focus on what is accomplished and record them.

☐ 4. Get some fresh ideas. Carve out some time and study something deeply, look for parallels outside your organization, find a good sounding board, talk to an expert in an unrelated field, talk to the most imaginative person you know, look for unusual facts that don't fit and ask what they might mean, use a storyboard to pictorially look at a problem or process.

☐ 5. Use some new thinking tools. Write down lists of pros and cons and then flowchart according to what's working and what isn't, run a scenario from A to Z, buy some planning software, look for the patterns in a problem rather than the solutions, convene a brainstorming session.

☐ 6. Maybe you give up too soon. If you have trouble persisting beyond the first try, switch approaches. Think about multiple ways to get to the same outcome. For example, you could meet with stakeholders first, bring in an expert to make the case, meet with a single key person to get feedback, or call a problem solving session and have the answer evolve from the discussion.

☐ 7. Too wrapped up in today? Don't like to speculate? Start reading international publications like the *Economist* and write down emerging trends. Research on the Internet topics that might affect your organization—see what leading thinkers are saying about them. Set a goal of coming up with three to five emerging trends.

☐ 8. Go against the grain. Fight sameness. Purposefully look outside the box. Look under the rocks for the new, different, and unique. Be outrageous and silly. Think like a child. Ask why again and again. Extend yourself. Be courageous and propose things at the margins.

☐ 9. **(Workaround)** Engage internal or external resources who enjoy and are good at looking under rocks. Get creative people to look at it for you. Have them dig and find as many things as they can before you spend time on it.

☐ 10. **(Workaround)** Hire someone for your staff or team who is creative and innovative. Give them the tasks that require digging deep and looking for the new and different. Give them time and resources. Be patient. Always recognize their efforts whether you use what they come up with or not.

MORE HELP?

See *FYI For Your Improvement*™. We have coded each item to about 10 tips from the *FYI* book. To use this resource, the codes below refer to the chapter and then the tip number from the *FYI* book. For example, in item 7 below, 1-5,6 refers to Chapter 1—Action Oriented, tips 5 and 6. If you don't have a copy of *FYI*, it is available through Lominger at 952-345-3610 or www.lominger.com

7. Is on the hunt for something new; seems to need fresh challenges.
1-5,6; 2-3; 6-3,4,6; 14-1, 43-1; 57-1; 118-8

34. Is more fascinated, amused, or intrigued with tough problems and challenges than stressed, troubled, or strained.
2-1,3; 14-1,2,9; 32-2,4; 51-1,4,8

61. Is a curious person; is intellectually adventuresome.
1-5; 14-1; 30-3,4; 32-9; 46-8,9; 51-1; 58-3; 118-8

JOBS THAT WOULD ADD SKILLS IN THIS DIMENSION

☐ Scope (very broad) Assignments—managing a high variety of activities at different levels of complexity and certainty.

☐ Start-ups—requiring doing a lot of first-time things and meeting new challenges that need fixing in a short period of time.

☐ Heavy Strategic Demands—finding the essence of a new direction.

☐ Line to Staff Switch—where you have to learn a new set of issues and problems in a new setting.

☐ Chair of Projects/Task Forces—where the issues are apt to be new and first-time challenges and those where you have to help others understand.

PART-TIME ASSIGNMENTS THAT WOULD ADD SKILLS IN THIS DIMENSION

☐ Work on a team fixing something that has failed.

☐ Work with a highly diverse team to accomplish a difficult task.

☐ Take on a tough and undoable project where others have failed.

☐ Relaunch an existing product/service that's not doing well.

☐ Launch a new product or service.

☐ Handle a tough negotiation with an external or internal customer, a union, a key vendor, or a dissatisfied customer.

☐ Work on a team managing a significant business crisis (workplace violence, Tylenol scare, Bhopal).

☐ Work on a multifunctional team trying to solve an issue that crosses boundaries in the organization.

☐ Plan a new site for a building or installation (plant, field office, headquarters, etc.).

☐ Work on a team that has to integrate diverse systems (move from using five computer platforms into one), processes (moving from ISO, TQM, and Six Sigma into only one of the three), or procedures (five competency models into one) across decentralized and/or dispersed units where you have to find the most common solution.

SUGGESTED READINGS

Bolles, Richard N. *What color is your parachute?* Berkeley, CA: Ten Speed Press, 2004.

De Bono, Edward. *Six thinking hats*. Boston: Little, Brown, 1985.

Epstein, Seymour, Ph.D. with Archie Brodsky. *You're smarter than you think—How to develop your practical intelligence for success in living*. New York: Simon & Schuster, 1993.

Glassman, Peter J. *J.S. Mill: The evolution of a genius*. Gainesville: University of Florida Press, 1985.

Hale, Guy. *The leader's edge—Mastering the five skills of breakthrough thinking*. Burr Ridge, IL: Irwin Professional Publishing, 1996.

Holton, Bill and Cher Holton. *The manager's short course: Thirty-three tactics to upgrade your career*. New York: John Wiley & Sons, 1992.

Peters, Tom. *Liberation management*. New York: Knopf, 1992.

DIMENSION 8
SOLUTION FINDER

SKILLED

Ingenious problem solver; can combine parts of ideas, come up with missing pieces, play with different combinations, etc.

UNSKILLED

May have one way or too lockstep a method of problem solving; may be unwilling to play with the puzzle before him/her.

ITEMS

- [ ] 8. Can combine the best parts of more than one idea or solution from multiple people and sources into a net better idea or solution.
- [ ] 35. Comes up with what's missing and can fill in the missing pieces as a method of getting information and solving problems.
- [ ] 62. Can play or fiddle with ideas to solve problems.

LEADERSHIP ARCHITECT® COMPETENCIES MOST ASSOCIATED WITH THIS DIMENSION

Strong

- [ ] 2. *Dealing with* Ambiguity
- [ ] 14. Creativity
- [ ] 46. Perspective
- [ ] 51. Problem Solving

Moderate

- [ ] 32. Learning on the Fly
- [ ] 52. Process Management

Light

- ☐ 33. Listening
- ☐ 40. *Dealing with* Paradox
- ☐ 41. Patience

SOME CAUSES

- ☐ Conventional
- ☐ Doesn't dig deep enough
- ☐ Doesn't take the time
- ☐ Fear of uncertainty
- ☐ Impatient
- ☐ Lacks curiosity
- ☐ Narrow background
- ☐ Not creative
- ☐ Not experimental
- ☐ Perfectionist
- ☐ Relies on the past
- ☐ Stops too soon
- ☐ Wants to get things done in a hurry

THE MAP

It's easy to fall into the habit of relying on our personal history. An experiment some years ago was abandoned because no one tried a new method to find a solution. Each person simply reached into his or her bag of solutions and pulled out another one. Unique, new, and different solutions fuel progress. The new, unique, and different takes some time, work, and skills to get to.

SOME REMEDIES

☐ 1. Get some fresh ideas. Carve out some time and study something deeply, look for parallels outside your organization, find a good sounding board, talk to an expert in an unrelated field, talk to the most imaginative person you know, look for unusual facts that don't fit and ask what they might mean, use a storyboard to pictorially look at a problem or process.

☐ 2. Use some new thinking tools. Write down lists of pros and cons and then flowchart according to what's working and what isn't, run a scenario from A to Z, buy some planning software, look for the patterns in a problem rather than the solutions, convene a brainstorming session.

☐ 3. Ask more questions. In one study of problem solving, 7 percent of comments were questions and about half were solutions. Others have shown that defining the problem and taking action occur almost simultaneously, so the more effort you put up front, the better. Stop and define what the problem is and isn't, what causes it, see how many organizing buckets you can put the causes in. This increases the chance of a better solution because you can see more possible connections among problem elements.

☐ 4. Don't go for the first solution. Studies show on average that either the second or the third solution generated is usually superior.

☐ 5. **(Workaround)** Read biographies of famous people who had to come up with critical solutions. Churchill, for example, always slept on an issue, no matter how urgent. Initially, he only asked questions to try to understand the issue. He kept his views to himself. See what you can learn from people you admire. A helpful Web site for finding biographical summaries, books, videos, etc. is www.biography.com. Additionally, they list a monthly schedule for the Biography Channel, a cable channel on the A&E network dedicated to biography shows and specials on significant lives.

☐ 6. Check for common errors in thinking. Do you state as facts things that are really opinions or assumptions? Do your feelings or emotions get in the way of issues? Do you attribute cause and effect to relationships when you don't know if one causes the other? Do you generalize from a single example? Do you treat factors as if they are equally important?

☐ 7. Think in opposite cases when confronted with a tough problem. Turn the problem upside down. Ask what is the least likely thing the problem could be, what the problem is and is not, what's missing from the problem that, if there, would lead to a solution, or what the mirror image of the problem is.

☐ 8. Try out some oddball tactics. What is a direct analogy between something you are working on and something in nature? Engineers once solved an overheating problem by drawing a parallel to what animal trainers do to calm upset or angry animals.

☐ 9. **(Workaround)** Engage internal or external resources who enjoy and are good at coming up with creative, unique, different and ingenious solutions to things. Let them work on it before you engage yourself.

☐ 10. **(Workaround)** Look to history for solutions. There are few really new problems. Look for parallel or similar situations. Log the solutions from the past. Test them out against the current issue.

MORE HELP?

See *FYI For Your Improvement*™. We have coded each item to about 10 tips from the *FYI* book. To use this resource, the codes below refer to the chapter and then the tip number from the *FYI* book. For example, in item 8 below, 14-2,3,4 refers to Chapter 14—Creativity, tips 2,3, and 4. If you don't have a copy of *FYI*, it is available through Lominger at 952-345-3610 or www.lominger.com

8. Can combine the best parts of more than one idea or solution from multiple people and sources into a net better idea or solution.
14-2,3,4; 17-3,5; 30-2; 32-2,3; 41-7; 101-3

35. Comes up with what's missing and can fill in the missing pieces as a method of getting information and solving problems.
14-2,3,4; 17-3,5; 30-2; 32-2,3,6; 101-3

62. Can play or fiddle with ideas to solve problems.
14-2,3,4; 17-3,5; 30-2; 32-2,3,6; 101-2

JOBS THAT WOULD ADD SKILLS IN THIS DIMENSION

☐ Scope (very broad) Assignments—managing a high variety of activities at different levels of complexity and uncertainty with problems galore to find solutions for.

☐ Heavy Strategic Demands—finding strategic solutions for tough marketplace challenges.

☐ Influencing Without Authority—finding solutions to tough problems with insufficient direct power to make anything happen with sensitive politics.

☐ Out of Home Country Assignments—where you are mostly on your own to find new or different solutions to tough problems in a different setting from your background.

☐ Start-ups—requiring finding solutions to first-time problems where there are no direct rules of thumb or reference points.

PART-TIME ASSIGNMENTS THAT WOULD ADD SKILLS IN THIS DIMENSION

☐ Work with a highly diverse team to accomplish a difficult task.

☐ Take on a tough and undoable project where others have failed to find the solution.

☐ Work on a team moving a group through an unpopular change.

☐ Work on a team fixing something that has failed.

- ☐ Relaunch an existing product/service that's not doing well.

- ☐ Work on a multifunctional team trying to solve an issue that crosses boundaries in the organization.

- ☐ Manage a dissatisfied internal or external customer; troubleshoot a performance or quality problem with a new product or service.

- ☐ Work on a team managing a significant business crisis (workplace violence, Tylenol scare, Bhopal).

- ☐ Handle a tough negotiation with an external or internal customer, a union, a key vendor, or a dissatisfied customer.

- ☐ Plan a new site for a building or installation (plant, field office, headquarters, etc.).

SUGGESTED READINGS

De Bono, Edward. *Six thinking hats*. Boston: Little, Brown, 1985.

Epstein, Seymour, Ph.D. with Archie Brodsky. *You're smarter than you think—How to develop your practical intelligence for success in living*. New York: Simon & Schuster, 1993.

Glassman, Peter J. *J.S. Mill: The evolution of a genius*. Gainesville: University of Florida Press, 1985.

Hale, Guy. *The leader's edge—Mastering the five skills of breakthrough thinking*. Burr Ridge, IL: Irwin Professional Publishing, 1996.

Kennedy, Paul M. *The rise and fall of the great powers: Economic change and military conflict from 1500 to 2000*. New York, NY: Random House, 1987.

The Systems Thinker®. Waltham, MA: Pegasus Communications, Inc., 781-398-9700.

HIGH

This Factor measures self-management in relationship to others. In one sense, it is related to the concept of EQ (Emotional Quotient) or EI (Emotional Intelligence). People high on this Factor know themselves better and are more open-minded toward others. They seek feedback and respond to it through personal change. In interactions with others, they are seen as helpful, constructive even in disagreement, and open to diversity of people and viewpoints. They are clear in presenting viewpoints to others and are good at explaining their thinking and that of others. They relate to others well.

LOW

People low on this Factor may not deploy themselves as well because they don't know themselves well: They over- or underestimate themselves and their skills, don't know their limits, or might mishandle situations that they think are being handled well. Lacking insight into self, they may lack it into others as well. Perhaps due to this, they might not handle conflict well, misreading or mishandling the situation. Leading change efforts may be a shortcoming due to some combination of inflexibility, lack of clear, calm transactions with others, political missteps, or not being seen as constructive with others.

SOME CAUSES

- ☐ Doesn't care about others
- ☐ Doesn't listen
- ☐ Gets frustrated and has a temper
- ☐ Gets stressed or overwhelmed easily
- ☐ Impatient

continued

- ☐ Misogynist or racist
- ☐ Narrow perspective
- ☐ Not in a feedback-rich situation
- ☐ Not observant
- ☐ Overly serious
- ☐ Resists feedback
- ☐ Self-centered
- ☐ Stuck in the past; prefers old ways
- ☐ Uncomfortable with face-to-face conflict
- ☐ Withdrawn or shy

Factor II

DIMENSION 9
AGILE COMMUNICATOR

SKILLED

Considers the audience; is articulate, can make the complex understandable; uses appropriate language to sell a view; fairly presents the arguments of others.

UNSKILLED

May be inarticulate, appeal to an audience incorrectly, or be unable to present a complex argument; may overwhelm the audience with emotion or detail; may not characterize the arguments of others well.

ITEMS

☐ 9. Can present ideas and concepts in the language of the target audience.

☐ 36. Can articulately explain complex ideas and concepts to others.

☐ 63. Is able to state opposing opinions and arguments clearly and without bias.

LEADERSHIP ARCHITECT® COMPETENCIES MOST ASSOCIATED WITH THIS DIMENSION

Strong

☐ 49. Presentation Skills

☐ 56. Sizing Up People

☐ 64. Understanding Others

Moderate

☐ 27. Informing

☐ 33. Listening

☐ 45. Personal Learning

☐ 51. Problem Solving

Light

- [ ] 12. Conflict Management
- [ ] 40. *Dealing with* Paradox
- [ ] 41. Patience
- [ ] 46. Perspective
- [ ] 47. Planning

SOME CAUSES

- [ ] Can't simplify
- [ ] Doesn't handle conflict calmly
- [ ] Doesn't listen
- [ ] Doesn't read people or audiences well
- [ ] Goes too fast for others to keep up
- [ ] Impatient
- [ ] Inflexible and rigid
- [ ] Intolerant of slower people
- [ ] Not good integrating technology for presentations
- [ ] Not humorous
- [ ] Not planful
- [ ] Not quick on the uptake
- [ ] Shoots from the hip

THE MAP

It's all in the communicating. Nothing is more of a lubricant than that. You have to be able to convey meaning. You have to be able to tell others what you know. You have to be able to adjust your pace, style, and message to the audience. Knowing it yourself is seldom enough. Conveying is success.

SOME REMEDIES

☐ 1. State your message or purpose in a single sentence, then outline your talk around three to five things that support this thesis and that you want people to remember. Consider what an audience member should say 15 minutes after you finish.

☐ 2. Don't try to tell the audience all you know, even if they are well-informed on the topic. You are giving a persuasive argument or communicating key information; it's not a lecture. Drowning people in detail will lose even the most knowledgeable and the interested.

☐ 3. Practice out loud. Writing out a pitch or argument isn't useful until you say it. Writing sounds stilted when spoken because the cadence of speech and sentence length is generally quite different.

☐ 4. Watch out for jargon if you have to explain something complex. Again, it's not a lecture. If you are speaking on a technical issue to a non-technical audience, present as if you were talking to a bright twelve year old. You're sure he or she will understand if you use straightforward language and logic.

☐ 5. Vary your presentation by audience. Some common questions to consider are: What's their time tolerance? How much do they expect to participate? Do they prefer formal or informal? Would they rather just chat about the topic? How sophisticated is the group? How much pushback do you expect?

☐ 6. Learn the language of different audiences. If you're a marketing person speaking with engineers, learn their conceptual categories by asking them how they would analyze it and what questions they would ask.

☐ 7. Minimize your presentation and maximize two-way exchange with the audience. Present your points in outline format and encourage maximum discussion and dialogue.

☐ 8. Make sure you know the points of view of others. Don't just tell and sell. Be able to clearly state their views.

☐ 9. **(Workaround)** For critical presentations, engage someone who is a proven communicator to present your message for you. You provide the input and the key points. You might also introduce the speaker and set the stage for the audience.

☐ 10. **(Workaround)** Use a recorded message. Have your presentation videotaped until it reaches standard judged by someone you trust. Have someone else manage the event and present the tape.

MORE HELP?

See *FYI For Your Improvement*™. We have coded each item to about 10 tips from the *FYI* book. To use this resource, the codes below refer to the chapter and then the tip number from the *FYI* book. For example, in item 9 below, 49-1,2,3,4,5 refers to Chapter 49—Presentation Skills, tips 1,2,3,4 and 5. If you don't have a copy of *FYI*, it is available through Lominger at 952-345-3610 or www.lominger.com

9. Can present ideas and concepts in the language of the target audience.
49-1,2,3,4,5; 64-8; 65-1,5; 67-3,4

36. Can articulately explain complex ideas and concepts to others.
2-5; 27-6; 32-1,2,3; 49-2; 51-1,5; 52-3; 65-1

63. Is able to state opposing opinions and arguments clearly and without bias.
12-1,2,3,4,5; 31-2; 33-7,8,9; 41-7

JOBS THAT WOULD ADD SKILLS IN THIS DIMENSION

☐ Out of Home Country Assignments—requiring communicating to a new and diverse population.

☐ Influencing Without Authority—communicating across organizational boundaries without the power to command attention.

☐ Scope (very broad) Assignments—requiring communicating to a variety of people about a variety of topics.

☐ Start-ups—requiring forging a new team and communicating on a variety of new and first-time subjects on a tight timetable.

☐ Significant People Demands—requiring communicating to a large number of people, usually in dispersed structures.

☐ Cross Moves—requiring communicating with a new group of people from another function.

☐ Line to Staff Switches—requiring communicating with a new group of people with different functional homes and a different viewpoint on the world.

PART-TIME ASSIGNMENTS THAT WOULD ADD SKILLS IN THIS DIMENSION

☐ Work on a team moving a balky and resisting group through an unpopular change or project.

☐ Build a multifunctional team to tackle an issue that crosses boundaries in the organization.

☐ Work on a team that has to integrate diverse systems (move from using five computer platforms into one), processes (moving from ISO, TQM, and Six Sigma into only one of the three), or procedures (five competency models into one) across decentralized and/or dispersed units where you have to find the most common solution.

☐ Work with a highly diverse team to accomplish a difficult task.

☐ Work on a team fixing something that has failed.

☐ Relaunch an existing product/service that's not doing well.

☐ Handle a tough negotiation with an external or internal customer, a union, a key vendor, or a dissatisfied customer.

☐ Manage a renovation project.

☐ Represent the concerns of one group to another where the groups are substantially different (clerical and senior management, union and non-union, one country to another).

☐ Be a change agent; create symbols for change; lead the way; champion a significant change.

SUGGESTED READINGS

Bolton, Robert and Dorothy Grover Bolton. *People styles at work.* New York: AMACOM, 1996.

Collins, Patrick J. *Say it with confidence.* New York: Prentice Hall, 1998.

Dimitrius, Jo-Ellan and Mark Mazzarella. *Reading people: How to understand people and predict their behavior—Anytime, anyplace.* New York: Random House, 1998.

Dowis, R. *The lost art of the great speech.* New York: AMACOM, 2000.

Kheel, Theodore W. *The keys to conflict resolution—Proven methods of resolving disputes voluntarily.* New York: Four Walls Eight Windows, 1999.

Kiser, A. Glenn. *Masterful facilitation: Becoming a catalyst for meaningful change.* New York: AMACOM, 1998.

Lee, John H. with Bill Stott. *Facing the fire: Experiencing and expressing anger appropriately.* New York: Bantam Books, 1993.

Presentations Magazine. www.presentations.com

Rafe, Stephen C. *How to be prepared to think on your feet.* New York: HarperBusiness, 1990.

6

DIMENSION 10
CONFLICT MANAGER

SKILLED

Constructive with others; knows how to handle conflicts and disagreements; watches others closely and adjusts.

UNSKILLED

May have problems dealing with conflict or seeing and explaining others' points of view; may not gauge impact on others well.

ITEMS

- ☐ 10. Even though he/she may not agree, understands and can explain the arguments and positions of others.
- ☐ 37. Can deal constructively with people he/she disagrees with, doesn't like, or is in conflict with on other issues.
- ☐ 64. Monitors others closely to gauge his/her impact and adjusts accordingly.

LEADERSHIP ARCHITECT® COMPETENCIES MOST ASSOCIATED WITH THIS DIMENSION

Strong

- ☐ 12. Conflict Management
- ☐ 33. Listening
- ☐ 56. Sizing Up People

Moderate

- ☐ 40. *Dealing with* Paradox
- ☐ 45. Personal Learning
- ☐ 51. Problem Solving
- ☐ 64. Understanding Others

Light

☐ 11. Composure

☐ 31. Interpersonal Savvy

☐ 32. Learning on the Fly

☐ 41. Patience

☐ 46. Perspective

SOME CAUSES

☐ Avoids conflict

☐ Defensive

☐ Doesn't listen

☐ Gets stressed and frustrated easily

☐ Has strong viewpoints on everything

☐ Holds grudges

☐ Impatient

☐ Inflexible or rigid

☐ Not observant

☐ Not open to personal diversity

☐ Opinionated

☐ Self-centered

☐ Strong need to dominate

☐ Wants to win at all costs

THE MAP

A recent survey revealed that managers spend 18 percent of their time dealing with face-to-face conflict. Most organizations are decentralized and compartmentalized which sets up natural conflict. Added to this is the accelerated pace of change where processes and procedures undergo near constant tweaking. Dealing with and resolving conflict is of increasing importance. There is nothing more certain than uncertainty and the conflict that comes from it.

SOME REMEDIES

☐ 1. Have to win every battle? Some of us cause unnecessary conflict with our language and attitude toward winning. Do you challenge others and offer solutions and opinions too early? Increase the perception of fairness by focusing on common-ground issues. Try to find wins for both sides. Give in on little points. Avoid starting with strong positions. Give reasons first and solutions last.

☐ 2. Keep conflicts small. Find out what the points of agreement are rather than focusing on the disagreements only. Don't resort to general statements such as "We have trust problems with your unit." Keep the concern specific—stick to the specific whats and whens.

☐ 3. Stay away from the personal. Sometimes our emotional reactions lead others to believe we can't handle conflict. Learn your telltale signs (Voice go up? Drum your fingers? Shift in your chair?) and substitute something more useful. Pause, take a deep breath, ask a question, rephrase something until you can respond appropriately. Stick to facts and problems; stay away from personalizing the issue.

☐ 4. Follow the rule of equity. Explain your thinking and ask others to explain theirs. Be able to state their opinions as clearly as they can. Generate a variety of possibilities rather than staking out a rigid position. Keep your voice calm and speak briefly. Practice asking more questions and making fewer statements.

☐ 5. Don't signal that you don't like someone or that they are wasting your time. Your goal should be to help and understand, not judge. Help others structure their arguments or be more concise. Focus on the strengths they have, not inevitable human shortcomings. Give second chances. Put your mind in neutral and ask questions.

☐ 6. Slow down. Impatient people provide solutions too early in the process. Take time to really define the problem and hear people out. Figure out what questions need to be answered in order to resolve it.

☐ 7. Monitor others. Watch the reactions of people to what you are doing or saying. If they're bored, change the pace. Confused? State your argument differently. Angry? Stop and find out what's going on. Too quiet? Ask a question; get them engaged. Disinterested? Figure out what's in it for them. Be ready to adjust.

☐ 8. What if you're attacked? Let the other side vent, but don't react directly. Listen. Nod. Ask clarifying questions. Ask open-ended questions like "What could I do to help?" Restate their position so they know you've heard them. You don't have to do anything to appease, just listen and accept that they are irritated. Your goal is to calm the situation so you can get back to more reasonable discussion.

☐ 9. **(Workaround)** Engage an internal or external resource who can help with conflict resolution. Have him/her visit with the parties involved and summarize the nature of the conflict. Have him/her also suggest a number of methods for resolving as much of the conflict as possible.

☐ 10. **(Workaround)** Use someone close to you (possibly on your staff) to alert you to upcoming conflicts. You might also have them suggest optional strategies to defuse the conflict before it escalates. Practice upcoming conflicts in your mind. Run through a number of possible scenarios.

MORE HELP?

See *FYI For Your Improvement™*. We have coded each item to about 10 tips from the *FYI* book. To use this resource, the codes below refer to the chapter and then the tip number from the *FYI* book. For example, in item 10 below, 12-1,2,3,4,5 refers to Chapter 12— Conflict Management, tips 1,2,3,4 and 5. If you don't have a copy of *FYI*, it is available through Lominger at 952-345-3610 or www.lominger.com

10. Even though he/she may not agree, understands and can explain the arguments and positions of others.
12-1,2,3,4,5; 31-2; 33-7,8,9; 41-7

37. Can deal constructively with people he/she disagrees with, doesn't like, or is in conflict with on other issues.
12-1,5,7; 33-7,9; 37-1,2; 41-7; 101-5; 104-4

64. Monitors others closely to gauge his/her impact and adjusts accordingly.
31-2,3; 45-1,2,3,4,5,6,7; 104-4

10

JOBS THAT WOULD ADD SKILLS IN THIS DIMENSION

☐ Out of Home Country Assignments—requiring conflicting cultures and a new and diverse population.

☐ Influencing Without Authority—communicating across organizational boundaries without the power to command attention where people and political skills are at a premium.

☐ Cross Moves—requiring working with a new group of people from another function with a different background and viewpoint.

☐ Fix-its/Turnarounds—requiring making tough decisions impacting a variety of people and constituencies.

☐ Line to Staff Switches—requiring working with a new group of people with different functional homes and a different viewpoint on the world.

PART-TIME ASSIGNMENTS THAT WOULD ADD SKILLS IN THIS DIMENSION

☐ Make peace with an enemy or someone you've disappointed or someone you've had some trouble with or don't get along with.

☐ Work on moving a balky and resisting group through an unpopular change or project.

☐ Help shut down a facility or office or territory and work on who to let go and who to keep.

☐ Handle a tough negotiation with an external or internal customer, a union, a key vendor, or a dissatisfied customer.

☐ Manage a dissatisfied internal or external customer; troubleshoot a performance or quality problem with a new product or service.

☐ Take on a tough and undoable project where others have failed before you and lots of other people are involved.

☐ Work on a team fixing something that has failed.

☐ Work with a highly diverse team to accomplish a difficult task.

☐ Work on a team that has to integrate diverse systems (move from using five computer platforms into one), processes (moving from ISO, TQM, and Six Sigma into only one of the three), or procedures (five competency models into one) across decentralized and/or dispersed units where you have to find the most common solution.

☐ Resolve a long-standing issue between groups where the groups are substantially different (clerical and senior management, union and non-union, one country to another).

SUGGESTED READINGS

Bolton, Robert. *People skills: How to assert yourself, listen to others and resolve conflicts.* New York: Simon & Schuster, 1986.

Bolton, Robert and Dorothy Grover Bolton. *People styles at work.* New York: AMACOM, 1996.

Burley-Allen, Madelyn. *Listening: The forgotten skill*. New York: John Wiley & Sons, 1995.

Dimitrius, Jo-Ellan and Mark Mazzarella. *Reading people: How to understand people and predict their behavior—Anytime, anyplace*. New York: Random House, 1998.

Dawson, Roger. *Secrets of power negotiating*. Franklin Lakes, NJ: Career Press, 1995.

Kheel, Theodore W. *The keys to conflict resolution—Proven methods of resolving disputes voluntarily*. New York: Four Walls Eight Windows, 1999.

Levine, Stewart. *Getting to resolution*. San Francisco: Berrett-Koehler Publishers, 1998.

Neuhauser, Peg. *Tribal warfare in organizations*. New York: Harper & Row, 1988.

Nichols, Michael P. *The lost art of listening*. New York: The Guilford Press, 1995.

Van Slyke, Erik J. *Listening to conflict*. New York: AMACOM, 1999.

10

10

DIMENSION 11
COOL TRANSACTOR

SKILLED

Unbiased; can easily state cases he or she disagrees with like an accomplished debater; accurate, fair, others will listen to what this person says.

UNSKILLED

May be alternately too passionate and one-sided or a poor listener/articulator of others' notions; at the extreme, may be viewed as overly self-sufficient and uncaring.

ITEMS

- ☐ 11. Uses objective and adjective-free language even when he/she feels strongly about things so as to not chill interactions.
- ☐ 38. Is good at delivering even negative feedback to others; can get others to listen.
- ☐ 65. Is politically adept; knows how to work with key decision makers and stakeholders.

LEADERSHIP ARCHITECT® COMPETENCIES MOST ASSOCIATED WITH THIS DIMENSION

Strong

- ☐ 11. Composure
- ☐ 12. Conflict Management
- ☐ 56. Sizing Up People
- ☐ 64. Understanding Others

Moderate

☐ 31. Interpersonal Savvy

☐ 36. Motivating Others

☐ 41. Patience

Light

☐ 2. *Dealing with* Ambiguity

☐ 8. Comfort Around Higher Management

☐ 13. Confronting Direct Reports

☐ 33. Listening

☐ 34. Managerial Courage

SOME CAUSES

☐ Avoids conflict

☐ Defensive

☐ Dislikes politics

☐ Doesn't listen

☐ Easily stressed or frustrated

☐ Holds grudges

☐ Impatient

☐ Inflexible

☐ Insensitive to others

☐ Intolerant of differences

☐ Opinionated

☐ Too personally involved

THE MAP

Turning down the volume and depersonalizing tough transactions are key aspects of persuasion and problem solving. Noise seldom helps. The brain turns down when the heat is turned up.

SOME REMEDIES

☐ 1. Go from specific to general points. Keep to the facts. Don't embellish and don't say everything you know or feel. If feelings are involved, wait until you can describe them, not show them.

☐ 2. Don't fool around. Don't waste time with a long preamble when the feedback is negative. If the recipient is likely to know what's coming, go ahead and say it directly. They won't hear anything positive until later anyway. If you have to be critical, you can still empathize with how he/she feels, and you can help with encouragement when the discussion turns more positive. Mentally rehearse these worst-case scenarios.

☐ 3. Have language problems? Use blaming, inflammatory words or do your words become impersonal and sterile? Either will blow the transaction for you. Speak to the person as you would like to be treated in the same situation. Avoid condescending terms like "What you need to understand" or "This is the third time...." Both imply the receiver is either stupid or unwilling. Keep your volume in the mid range. Avoid any critical or negative humor. While this may make you feel better, it will cut like a knife.

☐ 4. Describe problems, conditions, and impact. Don't pick words that are personal, blaming, or autocratic. Be more tentative and probabilistic. Keep all discussion specific. Don't generalize or use big words like "trust" or anything that impugns intelligence or suggests ill motives.

☐ 5. Eliminate poor habits, such as using the same words repeatedly, using filler words like "uh" and "you know," speaking too rapidly or forcefully, or going into so much detail that people can't follow the point. Outline arguments. Know the three things you're trying to say and say them succinctly. Others can always ask questions if something is unclear.

☐ 6. Work from the outside in. Determine the demands of the situation and select what style will play with a particular person or group. Think of any discussion as a quid pro quo. If you ask for help, what help can you provide in return. If people see you as competitive, they will cut you out of the loop. Establish common ground. Give in order to get.

☐ 7. Listen. Do you really know how others see the issue or do you tell and sell? Do you even know if it is important to them? Don't interrupt. Don't suggest words or solutions when they pause. Don't cut them off by saying "I already know that," "I've heard that before," or the dreaded "But that won't work." Help them say what they need to say.

☐ 8. Be an anthropologist. Learn what a group believes and why they believe this. What are their hot buttons? What's their goal? Nothing will kill you quicker with a group than to show utter disregard for their norms and views. Do your homework. If that's not possible, listen and ask lots of questions.

☐ 9. Rehearse what you need to say until you can say it without inflammatory or blameful language. Don't get caught having to deliver your message on the spur of the moment. Be planful. Pick your spots.

☐ 10. **(Workaround)** Engage an internal or external person to deliver the message you are having trouble delivering. Sometimes an HR professional might be used to pass on some corrective information you can't calmly handle. Or arrange a situation where the person will get the same message through some other method like a 360° or a course with feedback.

MORE HELP?

See *FYI For Your Improvement*™. We have coded each item to about 10 tips from the *FYI* book. To use this resource, the codes below refer to the chapter and then the tip number from the *FYI* book. For example, in item 11 below, 11-1,2,7,8 refers to Chapter 11— Composure, tips 1,2,7 and 8. If you don't have a copy of *FYI*, it is available through Lominger at 952-345-3610 or www.lominger.com

11. Uses objective and adjective free language even when he/she feels strongly about things so as to not chill interactions.
11-1,2,7,8; 12-2,5,7; 27-6; 41-1,2

38. Is good at delivering even negative feedback to others; can get others to listen.
12-3,5,7; 31-3,6; 34-1,3,4,10; 45-1

65. Is politically adept; knows how to work with key decision makers and stakeholders.
48-2,3,5,7; 64-5,6,8; 119-1,4,5

JOBS THAT WOULD ADD SKILLS IN THIS DIMENSION

☐ Fix-its/Turnarounds—requiring making tough decisions impacting a variety of people and constituencies.

☐ Crisis or Change Manager—requiring tough-minded decisions under tight time pressure with a low level of consultation.

☐ Influencing Without Authority—working across organizational boundaries without the power to command attention where people and political skills are at a premium; conflict cannot be resolved with authority; influence is the main tool.

☐ Start-ups—rapid decisions need to be made without much consultation.

☐ Significant People Demands—requiring a high volume of people decisions and transactions, many times without much consultation.

PART-TIME ASSIGNMENTS THAT WOULD ADD SKILLS IN THIS DIMENSION

☐ Work on moving a balky and resisting group through an unpopular change or project.

☐ Work on a team fixing something that has failed.

☐ Help shut down a facility or office or territory and work on who to let go and who to keep.

☐ Manage the outplacement of a number of people.

☐ Handle a tough negotiation with an external or internal customer, a union, a key vendor, or a dissatisfied customer.

☐ Manage a dissatisfied internal or external customer; troubleshoot a performance or quality problem with a new product or service.

☐ Manage the assigning/allocation of office space in a contested situation where everyone can't win or be satisfied.

☐ Resolve a long-standing issue between groups where the groups are substantially different (clerical and senior management, union and non-union, one country to another).

☐ Be a change agent; create symbols for change; lead the way; champion a significant change.

☐ Take on a tough and undoable project where others have failed before you and lots of other people are involved.

SUGGESTED READINGS

Bolton, Robert. *People skills: How to assert yourself, listen to others and resolve conflicts*. New York: Simon & Schuster, 1986.

Bolton, Robert and Dorothy Grover Bolton. *People styles at work*. New York: AMACOM, 1996.

Burley-Allen, Madelyn. *Listening: The forgotten skill*. New York: John Wiley & Sons, 1995.

Dawson, Roger. *Secrets of power negotiating*. Franklin Lakes, NJ: Career Press, 1995.

Dimitrius, Jo-Ellan and Mark Mazzarella. *Reading people: How to understand people and predict their behavior—Anytime, anyplace.* New York: Random House, 1998.

Kheel, Theodore W. *The keys to conflict resolution—Proven methods of resolving disputes voluntarily.* New York: Four Walls Eight Windows, 1999.

Kiser, A. Glenn. *Masterful facilitation: Becoming a catalyst for meaningful change.* New York: AMACOM, 1998.

Lee, John H. with Bill Stott. *Facing the fire: Experiencing and expressing anger appropriately.* New York: Bantam Books, 1993.

Levine, Stewart. *Getting to resolution.* San Francisco: Berrett-Koehler Publishers, 1998.

Neuhauser, Peg. *Tribal warfare in organizations.* New York: Harper & Row, 1988.

Nichols, Michael P. *The lost art of listening.* New York: The Guilford Press, 1995.

Van Slyke, Erik J. *Listening to conflict.* New York: AMACOM, 1999.

11

11

DIMENSION 12
HELPS OTHERS SUCCEED

SKILLED

Likes to see others do well; generous in credit and help.

UNSKILLED

May be too self-sufficient or uncaring; may envy the successes of others, fearing competition or being shown up; may see success as a zero-sum game.

ITEMS

- ☐ 12. Brings out the best in others; lets others shine and finds something they can contribute.
- ☐ 39. Is more a credit giver and sharer than a taker.
- ☐ 66. Generally likes others to succeed regardless of his/her personal evaluation or opinion of them.

LEADERSHIP ARCHITECT® COMPETENCIES MOST ASSOCIATED WITH THIS DIMENSION

Strong

- ☐ 18. Delegation
- ☐ 27. Informing
- ☐ 36. Motivating Others

Moderate

- ☐ 20. Directing Others
- ☐ 23. Fairness to Direct Reports
- ☐ 41. Patience

12

Light

- [ ] 19. Developing Direct Reports and Others
- [ ] 33. Listening
- [ ] 40. *Dealing with* Paradox
- [ ] 56. Sizing Up People
- [ ] 60. *Building Effective* Teams

SOME CAUSES

- [ ] A loner
- [ ] Doesn't take the time
- [ ] Doesn't understand people
- [ ] Excessively high standards
- [ ] Fear of failure
- [ ] Grandstander
- [ ] Insensitive
- [ ] Impatient
- [ ] Jealous of others
- [ ] Judgmental
- [ ] Selfish
- [ ] Short-term perspective
- [ ] Too competitive
- [ ] Unappreciative

THE MAP

Helping others, including your boss, succeed helps you succeed. There is a limited amount any of us can accomplish, regardless of how hard we work. Everyone knows this, but delegation and developing others are extremely weak skills in most organizations. Quite often we don't know how to help others succeed.

76

SOME REMEDIES

☐ 1. Why aren't you delegating? Are you a perfectionist, wanting everything to be just so? Unrealistic expectations? Won't risk giving out critical work? If this is you, expect career trouble. Better managers delegate more than managers who try to control most things. The keys are setting priorities, providing help, and designing work flows, not your personal effort.

☐ 2. How to delegate. Communicate, set time frames and goals, and get out of the way. Be very clear on what and when, be very open on how. People are more motivated when they can determine the how themselves. Encourage them to try things. Delegate complete tasks, not pieces. Allow more time than it would take you to do it.

☐ 3. Be a teacher. Always explain your thinking. Work out loud with them on a task. What do you see as important? How do you know? What questions are you asking? What steps are you following? Simply firing out solutions will make people more dependent at best.

12

☐ 4. Learn how to develop others. Developing direct reports and others is dead last in skill level among the 67 Competencies of the LEADERSHIP ARCHITECT® and has been since we started collecting these data. To develop people, you have to follow the essential rules of development. They take a bit of time. Development is not simply sending someone to a course:

- ■ Start with a portrait of the person's strengths and weaknesses. They can't grow if they are misinformed about themselves.

- ■ Provide ongoing feedback from multiple sources.

- ■ Give them progressively stretching tasks that are first-time and different for them. At least 70 percent of reported development occurs through challenging assignments that demand skill development. People don't grow from doing more of the same.

- Encourage them to think of themselves as learners, not just accomplishers. What are they learning that is new or different? What skills have improved in the last year? What have they learned that they can use in other situations?

- Use coursework, books, development partners, and mentoring to reinforce learning.

☐ 5. Follow the basic rules of motivating others. Communicate that what they do is important and how it's important. Offer help and ask for it. Provide autonomy and job challenge. Provide variety. Show an interest in their careers. Adopt a learning attitude toward mistakes. Celebrate successes. Set up reasonable goals that people can measure themselves against.

☐ 6. Be equitable. Don't use information as a reward for a few. Invite everyone's thinking, regardless of what you think of his or her level of performance. Turn off your judgment program and check to make sure you're not playing favorites or excusing behavior in a high performer that you wouldn't tolerate from anyone else. A neutral observer should not be able to tell from your demeanor who you favor and who you don't. Help the quiet, reserved and the shy have their say. Keep fairness conflicts small and concrete.

☐ 7. Do you promote the careers of others? Help others solve their problems, let others present and get the credit. Gain stature through the success of your people.

☐ 8. **(Workaround)** Set up a more formal reward and recognition system that is reasonably automatic and doesn't require you to stop and think about it. Install objective standards of fairness (performance standards, pay, office choices, days off).

☐ 9. **(Workaround)** Have your team manage rewards and recognition with your input and guidance. Let them decide on the standards and criteria and manage the selection process. Ask others around you for their opinions on who deserves rewards and recognition.

☐ 10. **(Workaround)** Keep a reward and recognition log for both hard (money) and soft (a positive comment). Try to balance the rewards among those you are responsible for, and try to hit everyone as often as you can.

MORE HELP?

See *FYI For Your Improvement*™. We have coded each item to about 10 tips from the *FYI* book. To use this resource, the codes below refer to the chapter and then the tip number from the *FYI* book. For example, in item 12 below, 18-1,5,8 refers to Chapter 18— Delegation, tips 1, 5, and 8. If you don't have a copy of *FYI*, it is available through Lominger at 952-345-3610 or www.lominger.com

12. Brings out the best in others; lets others shine and finds something they can contribute.
18-1,5,8; 19-1,2,3,4,6; 36-3,10

39. Is more a credit giver and sharer than a taker.
18-1; 36-1; 103-3,8,9; 104-4,6,7,8,9

66. Generally likes others to succeed regardless of his/her personal evaluation or opinion of them.
23-2,3,4,5; 103-3,8,9; 104-4,8,9

JOBS THAT WOULD ADD SKILLS IN THIS DIMENSION

☐ Significant People Demands—requiring managing a large number of people, including responsibility for their training and development.

☐ Fix-its/Turnarounds—requiring helping people rapidly change what they are doing and building their skills to be more successful.

☐ Scale (large) Assignments—managing larger numbers of people and being responsible for their current and future performance.

☐ Start-ups—requiring forging a new team and building new skills as you go.

PART-TIME ASSIGNMENTS THAT WOULD ADD SKILLS IN THIS DIMENSION

☐ Manage a group of green, novice, inexperienced, or new employees as their coach, teacher, mentor, or guide.

☐ Mange a group of people where you are the towering expert and they need to know what you do and be able to do what you do.

☐ Manage a group of low-competence people through a task they could not do by themselves.

☐ Work on moving a balky and resisting group through an unpopular change or project.

☐ Work on a team fixing something that has failed, where the same team who failed will stay to do it right.

☐ Work with a very diverse team of people to work on a tough issue none of them have done before, including you.

☐ Create employee involvement teams.

☐ Manage a group of people in a rapidly expanding unit that has to learn new things quickly.

☐ Build a multifunctional team to tackle an issue that crosses boundaries in the organization where no one person has all of the skills necessary to complete the task.

☐ Coach a sports team with new and inexperienced players (like youth soccer).

SUGGESTED READINGS

Bolton, Robert. *People skills: How to assert yourself, listen to others, and resolve conflicts.* New York: Simon & Schuster, 1986.

Daniels, Aubrey C. *Bringing out the best in people.* New York: McGraw-Hill, Inc., 1994.

Gilley, Jerry W. and Nathaniel W. Boughton. *Stop managing, start coaching.* Burr Ridge, IL: Irwin Professional Publishing, 1996.

Ginnodo, Bill. *The power of empowerment.* Arlington Heights, IL: Pride Publications, Inc., 1997.

Huppe, Frank T. *Successful delegation: How to grow your people, build your team, free up your time and increase profits and productivity*. Hawthorne, NJ: Career Press, 1994.

Nelson, Robert B. *Empowering employees through delegation*. Burr Ridge, IL: Irwin Professional Publishing, 1994.

Potts, Tom and Arnold Sykes. *Executive talent—Develop your best people*. Homewood, IL: Business One Irwin, 1993.

Stone, Florence M. *Coaching, counseling and mentoring*. New York: AMACOM, 1999.

12

12

SKILLED

Uses humor well; knows how to lighten things up.

UNSKILLED

May be too serious or not use comic relief to relieve tension.

ITEMS

- ☐ 13. Uses humor as a tool to get things done.
- ☐ 40. Can laugh at self.
- ☐ 67. Has fun at almost everything he/she does.

LEADERSHIP ARCHITECT® COMPETENCIES MOST ASSOCIATED WITH THIS DIMENSION

Strong

- ☐ 26. Humor
- ☐ 44. Personal Disclosure
- ☐ 45. Personal Learning

Moderate

- ☐ 11. Composure
- ☐ 12. Conflict Management
- ☐ 31. Interpersonal Savvy
- ☐ 46. Perspective
- ☐ 55. Self-Knowledge

Light

☐   3. Approachability

☐ 36. Motivating Others

☐ 56. Sizing Up People

☐ 57. Standing Alone

☐ 64. Understanding Others

SOME CAUSES

☐ Defensive and sensitive

☐ Doesn't see the humor in things

☐ Fear of being seen as silly

☐ Humorless

☐ Impatient

☐ Insensitive

☐ Low tolerance for diversity in style

☐ Low tolerance for uncertainty

☐ Overly serious

☐ Perfectionist

☐ Politically incorrect

☐ Shy or withdrawn

☐ Slow to catch on to humor

☐ Strong belief in separating personal from business

☐ Too planful and orderly

☐ Very private person

THE MAP

Humor and personal disclosure increase the involvement of others, make tough tasks seem more doable, relieve monotony, and contribute to a positive learning climate. Having a light touch can make a lot of things lighter for yourself and others.

SOME REMEDIES

☐ 1. Whether you're naturally funny or not, it's easy to use humor. It's in the news, in jokes, kids and pets, universal human foibles, a ridiculous situation you've been caught in lately. It's a question of tuning into and using what is around you.

☐ 2. Steer clear of political, ethnic, anything that makes fun of a whole group unless you're a member of that group, and angry humor. Some people use humor to deliver sarcastic messages like "Oh, thanks for telling me that," or "I would have never thought of that." Sarcastic humor puts down the person in a way that is hard to recover from, essentially indicating the person is a dodo for saying this.

☐ 3. Self-humor is usually safe. Funny stories about when you were embarrassed or about your latest household project that resulted in five trips to the hardware store or calling in an expert. Personal goofs humanize us to others.

☐ 4. Disclose more to others. Good kinds of disclosure are the reasons behind how you do or think about something at work, tidbits of important information you can share without breaching confidences, commentary about what's going on without being too negative about others, and what is coming up that will affect them. All of these build relationships and assist in performance.

☐ 5. Maybe you don't inform enough or are selective in informing. Informing is generally seen as an important skill that many people are not good at. When you see coworkers, ask yourself what you can share to help them do their jobs better.

☐ 6. Build a sense of fun for those around you. Parties, roasts, gag awards, and outings build cohesion. Start celebrating wins, honor those who have gone the extra mile, but don't honor anyone twice before everyone has been honored once. Working with the whole person tends to build teams.

☐ 7. Read *How to Be Funny* by Jon Macks, New York: Simon & Schuster, 2003.

☐ 8. **(Workaround)** Engage an internal or external speechwriter who is good at the lighter side. Have them suggest places for humorous quotes and cartoons that would lighten up your communications.

☐ 9. **(Workaround)** Delegate the fun planning to your staff. Let them plan the light and the humorous. Cooperate as best you can. Put on your happiest face.

☐ 10. **(Workaround)** Display cartoons in your workspace and in your presentations. Use them to set a tone and give others something light to comment on to break the ice.

MORE HELP?

See *FYI For Your Improvement*™. We have coded each item to about 10 tips from the *FYI* book. To use this resource, the codes below refer to the chapter and then the tip number from the *FYI* book. For example, in item 13 below, 26-1,2,3,4,5,6,7,8,9,10 refers to Chapter 26—Humor, tips 1–10. If you don't have a copy of *FYI*, it is available through Lominger at 952-345-3610 or www.lominger.com

13. Uses humor as a tool to get things done.
    26-1,2,3,4,5,6,7,8,9,10

40. Can laugh at self.
    26-1,3,7,8,9; 44-1,2,5,6; 60-7

67. Has fun at almost everything he/she does.
    1-6; 26-1,3,8,9,10; 44-1,2; 60-7; 118-8

JOBS THAT WOULD ADD SKILLS IN THIS DIMENSION

☐ Jobs are not a significant source of skill building in this area.

PART-TIME ASSIGNMENTS THAT WOULD ADD SKILLS IN THIS DIMENSION

☐ Help people write speeches with humor in them.

☐ Plan and run events (like off-sites) that have fun and silliness built into the activities.

☐ Be part of a team that puts on a humorous skit at a meeting.

☐ Volunteer to work for a charity or community organization to build your experiences with a broader spread of people.

☐ Work on a team that plans and carries out public relations activities or sales promotion events where some humor is present.

☐ Create and deliver a number of humorous stories about yourself at work and at play.

☐ Work on 10 self-humor statements or phrases you can use with people.

SUGGESTED READINGS

Adams, Scott. *The joy of work: Dilbert's guide to finding happiness at the expense of your co-workers* [sound recording]. New York: HarperCollins, 1998.

Antion, Tom. *Wake 'em up: How to use humor and other professional techniques to create alarmingly good business presentations*. Landover Hills, MD: Anchor Publications, 1997.

Barry, Dave. *Claw your way to the top* [sound recording]. Beverly Hills, CA: Dove Audio, 1993.

Dimitrius, Jo-Ellan and Mark Mazzarella. *Reading people: How to understand people and predict their behavior—Anytime, anyplace*. New York: Random House, 1998.

13

Dowse, Eileen. *The naked manager—How to build open relationships at work*. Greensboro, NC: Oakhill Press, 1998.

Fahlman, Clyde. *Laughing nine to five—The quest for humor in the workplace*. Portland, OR: Steelhead Press, 1997.

Hemsath, Dave and Leslie Yerkes. *301 Ways to have fun at work*. San Francisco: Berrett-Koehler Publishers, Inc., 1997.

Kheel, Theodore W. *The keys to conflict resolution—Proven methods of resolving disputes voluntarily*. New York: Four Walls Eight Windows, 1999.

Lee, John H. with Bill Stott. *Facing the fire: Experiencing and expressing anger appropriately*. New York: Bantam Books, 1993.

Linver, Sandy. *The leader's edge—How to use communication to grow your business and yourself*. New York: Simon & Schuster, 1994.

Macks, Jon. *How to be funny.* New York: Simon & Schuster, 2003.

13

DIMENSION 14
OPEN MINDED

SKILLED

Open to others, can change his/her mind; deals well with the differing actions and beliefs of others; open to new ideas, solutions.

UNSKILLED

Only or most comfortable with those most like him/her; not particularly open to different viewpoints; probably prefers tried-and-true solutions.

ITEMS

☐ 14. Is tolerant of diversity in thought, actions, beliefs, and behaviors.

☐ 41. Is comfortable managing diversity in others.

☐ 68. Free from past solutions or the way things have usually been done; approaches current problems with an open mind.

LEADERSHIP ARCHITECT® COMPETENCIES MOST ASSOCIATED WITH THIS DIMENSION

Strong

☐ 2. *Dealing with* Ambiguity

☐ 46. Perspective

Moderate

☐ 21. *Managing* Diversity

☐ 32. Learning on the Fly

☐ 33. Listening

☐ 64. Understanding Others

Light

☐ 12. Conflict Management

☐ 14. Creativity

☐ 51. Problem Solving

☐ 56. Sizing Up People

SOME CAUSES

☐ Doesn't listen

☐ Doesn't take the time

☐ Fear of the unknown

☐ High standards

☐ Impatient

☐ Inflexible or rigid

☐ Low tolerance of diversity

☐ Narrow background

☐ Not observant

☐ One best solution

☐ Opinionated

☐ Perfectionist

☐ Set in past ways

☐ Too conventional

THE MAP

Better learners collect more viewpoints and are more open to ideas and actions they don't necessarily agree with or want to do. The issue is what I can learn or gain from this, not what I personally care to do or believe. Open leads to more, closed to less.

SOME REMEDIES

☐ 1. Heterogeneous or diverse groups are more innovative than homogeneous groups. The findings indicate that the more variety in the group, the fresher the ideas. Pick five people not like you (in specialty, level, gender/ethnic group, background, history) and get to know how they think about the problems you face.

☐ 2. Avoid putting people in buckets of those who can help you and those who can't. Once you do that, the good bucket will get most of your attention. To break out of this, work on understanding without judging. Ask more questions, be a detective. You'll be pleasantly surprised at what you can gain from talking with people you don't ordinarily spend much effort on.

☐ 3. To deal effectively with any person or group, establish the rule of reciprocity. Relationships don't last unless you provide something and so do they. Find out what they want and tell them what you want. Learn how they think, what their conceptual categories are, what key factors they look at, and what kinds of questions they ask. Pick something in their argument that you agree with and reinforce this. All of these expand your thinking.

☐ 4. Avoid being a know-it-all. Nothing says closed to others like solution-minded, seen-it-all-before behavior. By all means, lay out your thinking and explore alternatives, but don't make closing statements too early. You'll learn basically nothing from others.

☐ 5. Manage the first three minutes. This is the key time to be open and approachable. Take in information, feel people out, listen. Don't come on strong because you're busy. Some key tests for this:

- Are you an early knower of information?
- Do people give you lots of information and ideas?
- Are people willing to do things for or with you?
- Open, approachable people get more done.
- Talk later than you usually do.

☐ 6. Define the problem, not the solution. Engage others in the whys, whats, and hows of what you are working on. Generate multiple solutions, don't settle on the first one. Be more aware of your biases. Do you drag out favorite solutions or reject anything that will force you to have to read a lot or interact with new people a lot? Go against your natural grain to be more open to different problem solving techniques.

☐ 7. Expand your network. Use people as sounding boards, convene a one-time problem solving group, or find a buddy group in another function or organization that faces a similar problem.

☐ 8. Try to think through or even present the viewpoints of the opposition. How did they form those viewpoints? If you were in their shoes, would you have come to the same conclusion? What do they not know that prevented them from coming to your conclusion? What have you learned by coldly examining their viewpoints that might change yours?

☐ 9. **(Workaround)** Use a formal exercise system like DeBono's Six Hats of Thinking (*Serious Creativity*, New York: HarperBusiness, 1992) to help facilitate you and your group through tough issues. Use the Myers-Briggs Type Indicator to help you and your group understand how each person functions and processes information and to teach you and the group about diversity of style.

☐ 10. **(Workaround)** Check your viewpoints with a disinterested person first before you disclose them. Find someone you trust who has no stake in the issue. Test out your viewpoint to check for bias.

MORE HELP?

See *FYI For Your Improvement*™. We have coded each item to about 10 tips from the *FYI* book. To use this resource, the codes below refer to the chapter and then the tip number from the *FYI* book. For example, in item 14 below, 21-6 refers to Chapter 21—*Managing Diversity*, tip 6. If you don't have a copy of *FYI*, it is available through Lominger at 952-345-3610 or www.lominger.com

14. Is tolerant of diversity in thought, actions, beliefs, and behaviors.
21-6; 31-1,2,3,4; 64-6,8,9; 101-4; 104-4

41. Is comfortable managing diversity in others.
21-1,2,5,6,8; 23-2; 64-5,6; 101-4,5

68. Free from past solutions or the way things have usually been done; approaches current problems with an open mind.
14-1; 51-1,2,3,5,8; 101-2,3,4; 118-8

JOBS THAT WOULD ADD SKILLS IN THIS DIMENSION

☐ Out of Home Country Assignments—requiring conflicting cultures and a new and diverse population.

☐ Cross Moves—requiring working with a new group of people from another function with a different background and viewpoint.

☐ Significant People Demands—requiring managing a large number of people, including responsibility for their training and development.

☐ Fix-its/Turnarounds—requiring helping people rapidly change what they are doing and building their skills to be more successful.

PART-TIME ASSIGNMENTS THAT WOULD ADD SKILLS IN THIS DIMENSION

☐ Assemble a team of diverse people to accomplish a difficult task.

☐ Integrate diverse systems, processes, or procedures across a decentralized or dispersed unit.

☐ Form a multifunctional team to tackle a common issue.

☐ Be a member of a union-negotiating or grievance-handling team.

☐ Resolve a conflict between two people or two units.

☐ Manage the renovation of an office, floor, building, warehouse, etc.

☐ Create and manage employee involvement teams.

☐ Handle customer complaints and suggestions.

☐ Manage a team of multinationals solving a common problem.

☐ Lobby for your organization on a contested issue in local, regional, state, federal, or international government.

SUGGESTED READINGS

Bolton, Robert. *People skills: How to assert yourself, listen to others and resolve conflicts.* New York: Simon & Schuster, 1986.

Bolton, Robert and Dorothy Grover Bolton. *People styles at work.* New York: AMACOM, 1996.

Burley-Allen, Madelyn. *Listening: The forgotten skill.* New York: John Wiley & Sons, 1995.

De Bono, Edward. *Serious creativity: Using the power of lateral thinking to create new ideas.* New York: HarperBusiness, 1992.

Firestine, Roger L., Ph.D. *Leading on the creative edge—Gaining competitive advantage through the power of creative problem solving.* Colorado Springs, CO: Piñon Press, 1996.

Kheel, Theodore W. *The keys to conflict resolution—Proven methods of resolving disputes voluntarily.* New York: Four Walls Eight Windows, 1999.

Leach, Joy with Bette George, Tina Jackson and Arleen Labella. *A practical guide to working with diversity—The process, the tools, the resources.* New York: AMACOM, 1995.

Levine, Stewart. *Getting to resolution.* San Francisco: Berrett-Koehler Publishers, 1998.

Neuhauser, Peg. *Tribal warfare in organizations.* New York: Harper & Row, 1988.

Nichols, Michael P. *The lost art of listening.* New York: The Guilford Press, 1995.

14

SKILLED

Interested in what people have to say; pays attention; is good at sizing up people.

UNSKILLED

May misread others; may have trouble seeing their strengths and weaknesses clearly; people's views may not have much impact on him/her.

ITEMS

☐ 15. Can empathize (put him/herself in the shoes of others).

☐ 42. Seems to get something out of interacting with others; works to gain from interactions.

☐ 69. Makes quick and mostly accurate judgments about people.

LEADERSHIP ARCHITECT® COMPETENCIES MOST ASSOCIATED WITH THIS DIMENSION

Strong

☐ 21. *Managing* Diversity

☐ 51. Problem Solving

☐ 56. Sizing Up People

Moderate

☐ 32. Learning on the Fly

☐ 33. Listening

☐ 64. Understanding Others

Light

- ☐ 2. *Dealing with* Ambiguity
- ☐ 36. Motivating Others
- ☐ 46. Perspective
- ☐ 55. Self-Knowledge

SOME CAUSES

- ☐ Doesn't care about others
- ☐ Doesn't listen
- ☐ Doesn't take the time
- ☐ Excessively high standards
- ☐ Impatient
- ☐ Narrow people background
- ☐ No interest in people
- ☐ No need for people
- ☐ Not curious
- ☐ Not observant
- ☐ Sees people in too simple terms
- ☐ Self-centered
- ☐ Too critical
- ☐ Too quick to judge
- ☐ Uses stereotypes

THE MAP

A key skill at any level is figuring out what people's strengths and weaknesses are so you can gain from their strengths and either help them develop or learn to discount their views in their weak or flat areas. Predicting what people will do in certain situations makes you better able to adjust and respond. Knowing people well leads to selecting better people. Knowing what people can do makes you a better manager. There's no downside to being able to read people.

SOME REMEDIES

☐ 1. Avoid generalizing about others. Just because someone is inept at their job doesn't mean they don't know how to do a hundred things better than you do. Just because someone is a star doesn't mean they don't have weaknesses.

☐ 2. Watch out for those you feel most comfortable with. They are likely to be similar in personality, political views, and skill set. There's not as much you can learn from an echo of yourself. Seek out variety, people who grate on you or whom you often disagree with. Work on understanding what they do well and not well. Turn off your judgment program.

☐ 3. Showing that you care is a good way to come to know others. Hear people out, find out what drives people and what their career aspirations are. Find out what you have in common. Give in order to get. Share the same information about yourself.

☐ 4. Follow the rules of listening. Don't interrupt, don't finish sentences, don't wave off further input by saying you already know something. Ask more questions if you want to learn to size up people better.

☐ 5. See if you can write down three specific strengths and three specific weaknesses for everyone you work with closely, then decide how sure you are of this assessment. You will probably be quite sure for people who are more like you or whom you have a personal relationship with, and less sure for those more remote. Spend time with all the people on your list until you feel comfortable that you know three true strengths and three need areas for everyone.

☐ 6. Learn a competency model. There are five or more validated descriptions of work behaviors that are related to performance. Use the categories of experts, not your homegrown ones, to size up people. Test the model against people you have worked with

99

closely across time (some you may no longer work with). See if you can differentiate the more from the less talented using this model. What strengths did both groups have in common? Which were different? What weaknesses did they share? Which were different? Use this to become less personal in your talent assessment. Most of us have characteristics we value (too much), downsides we excuse, and weaknesses we think are killers. Human competence is much more complex than our personal views. Learn to differentiate key competencies from the competencies that most people already have (basic intelligence, action orientation) and from the ones that are more likely to make a difference (such as sizing up people, dealing with ambiguity).

☐ 7. Observe more. See if you can predict what people are going to say and do before they do it. See if their behavior shows a pattern. See when they surprise you. By observing people more carefully, you get two benefits: You know their strengths and weaknesses better, and you can better adjust to their responses.

☐ 8. **(Workaround)** Rely on an internal or external person who is a known accurate evaluator of people. Or poll a number of people you respect who tend to be more accurate than you are for their opinions before you settle in to a viewpoint.

☐ 9. **(Workaround)** Use formal assessment. Use assessment centers, 360° feedback, simulations, a psychologist, or testing to get a more formal opinion about others.

☐ 10. **(Workaround)** Use assisted assessment. Use a questionnaire, a sort card competency deck, a piece of software, or a set of structured questions to help you structure your assessments of key people around you.

100

MORE HELP?

See *FYI For Your Improvement*™. We have coded each item to about 10 tips from the *FYI* book. To use this resource, the codes below refer to the chapter and then the tip number from the *FYI* book. For example, in item 15 below, 7-1,2,3,4,5,6,8 refers to Chapter 7—Caring about Direct Reports, tips 1,2,3,4,5,6 and 8. If you don't have a copy of *FYI*, it is available through Lominger at 952-345-3610 or www.lominger.com

15. Can empathize (put him/herself in the shoes of others).
7-1,2,3,4,5,6,8; 10-6,8,10

42. Seems to get something out of interacting with others; works to gain from interactions.
31-3,5,8,10; 33-3,6,9; 101-2,3,5

69. Makes quick and mostly accurate judgments about people.
33-4,5; 45-7; 56-1,3,4,6,7; 111-1,3

JOBS THAT WOULD ADD SKILLS IN THIS DIMENSION

☐ Out of Home Country Assignments—requiring conflicting cultures and a new and diverse population.

☐ Cross Moves—requiring working with a new group of people from another function with a different background and viewpoint.

☐ Significant People Demands—requiring managing a large number of people, including responsibility for their training and development.

☐ Influencing Without Authority—working across organizational boundaries without the power to command attention where people and political skills are at a premium; conflict cannot be resolved with authority; influence is the main tool.

☐ Start-ups—requiring forging a new team and building new skills as you go.

PART-TIME ASSIGNMENTS THAT WOULD ADD SKILLS IN THIS DIMENSION

☐ Be a member of a union-negotiating or grievance-handling team.

☐ Assemble a team of diverse people to accomplish a difficult task.

☐ Help shut down a plant, office, product line, business, operation, etc.

☐ Resolve a conflict between two people or two units.

☐ Manage a team of multinationals solving a common problem.

☐ Handle a tough negotiation with an internal or external client or customer.

☐ Integrate diverse systems, processes, or procedures across a decentralized or dispersed unit.

☐ Train and work as an assessor in an assessment center.

☐ Represent to higher management the concerns of a group of nonexempt, clerical, administrative, or union employees to seek a resolution of a difficult issue.

☐ Be a member of the campus interviewing team.

☐ Do a study of highly successful managers and contrast that to managers who have failed in your organization, including interviewing people who know or knew them, and report your findings to top management.

SUGGESTED READINGS

Autry, James A. *The art of caring leadership*. New York: William Morrow and Company, Inc., 1991.

Bolton, Robert. *People skills: How to assert yourself, listen to others and resolve conflicts*. New York: Simon & Schuster, 1986.

Bolton, Robert and Dorothy Grover Bolton. *People styles at work*. New York: AMACOM, 1996.

Burley-Allen, Madelyn. *Listening: The forgotten skill*. New York: John Wiley & Sons, 1995.

Daniels, Aubrey C. *Bringing out the best in people*. New York: McGraw-Hill, Inc., 1994.

Dimitrius, Jo-Ellan and Mark Mazzarella. *Reading people: How to understand people and predict their behavior—Anytime, anyplace*. New York: Random House, 1998.

Kummerow, Jean M., Nancy J. Barger and Linda K. Kirby. *Work types*. New York: Warner Books, 1997.

Leach, Joy with Bette George, Tina Jackson and Arleen Labella. *A practical guide to working with diversity—The process, the tools, the resources*. New York: AMACOM, 1995.

Smart, Bradford D., Ph.D. *Topgrading: How leading companies win by hiring, coaching, and keeping the best people*. New York: Prentice Hall, Inc., 1999.

15

15

DIMENSION 16
PERSONAL LEARNER

SKILLED

A continuous improver; actively seeks personal learning and skill building.

UNSKILLED

May be comfortable with current skills; at the extreme may fear the missteps that go with growth or be afraid to tackle personal projects.

ITEMS

- ☐ 16. Seeks and looks forward to opportunities for new learning experiences in business or personal areas.
- ☐ 43. Finds new things to learn and get good at.
- ☐ 70. Actively seeks out role models, living or dead, real or fictional, that can be helpful in learning or problem solving.

LEADERSHIP ARCHITECT® COMPETENCIES MOST ASSOCIATED WITH THIS DIMENSION

Strong

- ☐ 32. Learning on the Fly
- ☐ 45. Personal Learning
- ☐ 46. Perspective
- ☐ 54. Self-Development

Moderate

- ☐ 2. *Dealing with* Ambiguity
- ☐ 12. Conflict Management
- ☐ 51. Problem Solving

16

Light

- ☐ 33. Listening
- ☐ 55. Self-Knowledge
- ☐ 56. Sizing Up People

SOME CAUSES

- ☐ Comfortable with what is
- ☐ Doesn't see consequences
- ☐ Doesn't take the time
- ☐ Fear of failure
- ☐ Given up
- ☐ Happy and satisfied
- ☐ Impatient
- ☐ Lack of ambition
- ☐ Lack of self-awareness
- ☐ Lazy
- ☐ Low risk taker
- ☐ Low standards of excellence
- ☐ Not curious
- ☐ Not inspired
- ☐ Rigid and inflexible
- ☐ Stuck in the past

THE MAP

Learning new skills is a prime predictor of promotion and career success. Being an eager learner has been related to everything from sales success to level attained in organizations. The world is bigger for active learners.

SOME REMEDIES

☐ 1. Lost your passion for the job? Make a list of what you like to do and don't like to do. Concentrate on doing a few things you like each day. See if you can delegate or trade for more desirable activities. Do your least preferred activities first. Focus not on the activity but your sense of accomplishment. Volunteer for task forces and projects that would be more interesting for you.

☐ 2. Get out of your comfort zone. Find an activity that goes against your natural likes and try it. Up your risk comfort. Start small so you can recover quickly. Pick a few smaller tasks or challenges and build the skill bit by bit. For example, if strategy is your area, write a strategic plan for your unit and show it to people to get feedback, then write a second draft. Devise a strategy for turning one of your hobbies (i.e., photography) into a business.

☐ 3. Use your strengths to grow in new areas. If you are planful, plan how you will attack a new area. If you are interpersonally smooth, imagine yourself using your contacts and your network to learn something new.

☐ 4. Maybe you don't know your strengths and weaknesses well enough. Get a full 360° feedback from multiple sources and follow up with boss and human resources to see where you most need to improve.

☐ 5. Show others you take your development seriously. State your development needs and ask for help. Research shows that people are much more likely to help and think favorably of those who admit their shortcomings.

☐ 6. Try some new learning techniques. Many excellent learners have a grab bag of tactics. They ask lots of questions, save any solution statements for last, look outside their current line of work for parallels, keep a learning journal to capture insights, and so on.

☐ 7. Be more adventuresome. Travel to places you have not been before, go to ethnic festivals and talk to participants about their

16

culture, scan the newspaper for events in your area you have never attended. Serve with a community group, volunteer.

☐ 8. At work, pick three tasks you've never done before and go do them. For example, if you don't know much about customers, work in a store or handle complaints; get placed on task forces that will require new learning for you.

☐ 9. Seek out role models. Access great minds like John Stuart Mill on problem solving, or read a biography of Lyndon Johnson to learn about persuasion. Find three people who are excellent at something you want to develop in. Observe them, interview them, and see what they do that you do not. Ask them to think through an issue with you, what questions they would ask, and what they think good sources of knowledge are.

☐ 10. **(Workaround)** Think of yourself as an actor. An actor acts the part needed to make the play or movie work. Who they are is less important. Who they need to be is most important. Think about each key situation. How would Russell Crowe or Julia Roberts play the part? Body language? Voice? Pace? Process? Reactions? What are you trying to accomplish? What parts of you would work the best. See what works and what doesn't work.

MORE HELP?

See *FYI For Your Improvement*™. We have coded each item to about 10 tips from the *FYI* book. To use this resource, the codes below refer to the chapter and then the tip number from the *FYI* book. For example, in item 16 below, 1-6 refers to Chapter 1—Action Oriented, tip 6. If you don't have a copy of *FYI*, it is available through Lominger at 952-345-3610 or www.lominger.com

16. Seeks and looks forward to opportunities for new learning experiences in business or personal areas.
1-6; 14-1; 32-4; 45-6,7,8; 54-1,10; 57-9; 118-8

43. Finds new things to learn and get good at.
1-6; 46-1,5,7,8,9,10; 58-3; 61-7; 118-8

70. Actively seeks out role models, living or dead, real or fictional, that can be helpful in learning or problem solving.
1-6; 6-2; 30-10; 32-5; 46-2,3,6,8; 103-5; 118-8

JOBS THAT WOULD ADD SKILLS IN THIS DIMENSION

☐ Scope (very broad) Assignments—requiring communicating to a variety of people about a variety of topics.

☐ Out of Home Country Assignments—requiring conflicting cultures and a new and diverse population.

☐ Cross Moves—requiring working with a new group of people from another function with a different background and viewpoint.

☐ Heavy Strategic Demands—requiring significant strategic thinking and planning which charts new ground, along with selling it to a critical audience.

☐ Start-ups—requiring forging a new team and building new skills as you go.

PART-TIME ASSIGNMENTS THAT WOULD ADD SKILLS IN THIS DIMENSION

☐ Assemble a team of diverse people to accomplish a difficult task.

☐ Take on a tough and previously undoable project where others have tried but failed to come up with the right answer.

☐ Manage a group or a team of people who are towering experts in something you are not.

☐ Make peace with an enemy or someone you've disappointed with a product or service, or someone you've had some trouble with or don't get along well with.

☐ Teach a course, seminar, or workshop on something you don't know well.

☐ Attend a self-awareness workshop that has 360° and live feedback.

□   Handle a tough negotiation with an internal or external client or customer.

□   Integrate diverse systems, processes, or procedures across a decentralized or dispersed unit.

□   Help shut down a plant, office, product line, business, operation, etc.

□   Go on a business trip to a foreign country you've not been to before.

□   Manage a team of multinationals solving a common problem.

SUGGESTED READINGS

Bernstein, Albert J. and Sydney Craft Rozen. *Sacred bull: The inner obstacles that hold you back at work and how to overcome them*. New York: Wiley, 1994.

Bolles, Richard N. *What color is your parachute?* Berkeley, CA: Ten Speed Press, 2004.

Conger, Jay A. *Learning to lead*. San Francisco: Jossey-Bass, Inc., 1992.

Holton, Bill and Cher Holton. *The manager's short course: Thirty-three tactics to upgrade your career*. New York: John Wiley & Sons, 1992.

Kraus, Peter (Editor). *The book of leadership wisdom*. New York: John Wiley & Sons, 1998.

Lombardo, Michael and Robert Eichinger. *The leadership machine*. Minneapolis: Lominger, 2002.

Prochaska, James O., John C. Norcross and Carlo C. DiClemente. *Changing for good*. New York: Avon Books, 1995.

Stone, Florence M. and Randi T. Sachs. *The high-value manager —Developing the core competencies your organization needs*. New York: AMACOM, 1995.

DIMENSION 17
RESPONDS TO FEEDBACK

SKILLED

Comfortable with personal change, isn't paralyzed by mistakes; seeks feedback and moves on.

UNSKILLED

Closed, low interest in feedback or change; may deny or minimize mistakes and shortcomings. At the extreme, may be seen as self-important or, alternately, reticent.

ITEMS

☐ 17. Seeks feedback.

☐ 44. Is insightful about personal mistakes and failures; learns from them and moves on.

☐ 71. Have seen this person substantially change based upon critical feedback, making a mistake, or learning something new.

LEADERSHIP ARCHITECT® COMPETENCIES MOST ASSOCIATED WITH THIS DIMENSION

Strong

☐ 45. Personal Learning

☐ 54. Self-Development

Moderate

☐ 12. Conflict Management

☐ 33. Listening

☐ 55. Self-Knowledge

☐ 56. Sizing Up People

Light

- ☐ 2. *Dealing with* Ambiguity
- ☐ 32. Learning on the Fly
- ☐ 44. Personal Disclosure
- ☐ 51. Problem Solving
- ☐ 57. Standing Alone

SOME CAUSES

- ☐ Avoids conflict
- ☐ Avoids feedback
- ☐ Believes he/she's perfect
- ☐ Defensive
- ☐ Doesn't invite people in
- ☐ Doesn't listen
- ☐ Doesn't read others well
- ☐ Doesn't trust others
- ☐ Hard to approach
- ☐ Not ambitious
- ☐ Quick to blame others
- ☐ Rigid and inflexible
- ☐ Shy and withdrawn

THE MAP

Others view people who seek critical feedback more positively. People who seek positive feedback get the opposite response. The former shows willingness to improve. The latter is often seen as defensiveness and a disinterest in really knowing oneself. People who know themselves better do better. People who seek out feedback get more. Remember, whether you ask or not, everyone around has an opinion. Better to know.

SOME REMEDIES

☐ 1. Get more feedback. People who don't know their strengths and weaknesses tend to overestimate themselves, a consistent finding in the research literature that has been related to both poor performance and being terminated. 360° feedback, where you compare your responses on a set of competencies to those of boss, peers, direct reports (if any), and sometimes customers is the preferred approach. Many other avenues are open to you as well—boss, confidantes, or a development partner if you're lucky enough to have one.

☐ 2. Focus on the highest and lowest ratings from each group. Don't spend time worrying about whether your scores are high or low in an absolute sense. 360° instruments aren't designed as performance assessments ordinarily. For development, you should worry about you relative to you. What are your highest and lowest ratings?

☐ 3. Ask why. Why am I seen this way? How did my strengths get to be so? Are my weaknesses things I avoid, am simply not skilled at, things I dislike or things I've never done? What experiences shaped my pattern? Do I have strengths that are related to my weaknesses, such as the smart person who makes others feel less so? Use this analysis to determine what is relatively easier and tougher for you to do.

☐ 4. Follow up. Prepare specific areas you are concerned about and ask people to respond in writing. Ask them what they would like to see you keep doing, start doing, stop doing, or do differently. If you know the people well, you can try face-to-face feedback, although you should know that this is usually blander and more positive than written feedback. If you do this, select specific areas and state what you think the issue or need for improvement is. Don't ask general questions. Get them to respond to your statements.

☐ 5. Seen as arrogant and/or defensive? Many people with a need in this area are seen as self-sufficient and disinterested in feed-

113

back and change. If this is the case, you may have to ask repeatedly. And regardless of the feedback, accept it. Don't say it's inaccurate or a one-time failing; don't argue or qualify. Just take it in. Use mental rehearsal to get ready for what may happen. If you comment at all, give examples of the behavior being described to validate what they are saying. Chances are good they are right. Defensive and arrogant people typically have major blind spots.

☐ 6. Even if the feedback is not true, you need to deal with it. If people, especially those above you, believe these things, your career will be damaged. You need to construct a plan to convince people of the untruth(s) by deeds, not words. Plan how you will act in critical situations, and expect it to take quite a while for people to see you differently. It may take 10 times before people reconsider their view of you.

☐ 7. Disclose more. If you deny, minimize, or excuse away mistakes and shortcomings, take a chance and admit that you're imperfect like everyone else. Let your inside thoughts out in the open more often. Sprinkle normal work conversation with doubts, what you're thinking about and what's getting in the way. Since you probably don't know how to do this, select three people who are good at admitting mistakes and shortcomings and observe how they do it.

☐ 8. Take responsibility. Admit mistakes matter-of-factly, inform everyone potentially affected, learn from it so the mistake isn't repeated, then move on. Dwelling on the past is useless. Build up your heat shield. Successful people make lots of mistakes. Being right much more than two-thirds of the time is impossible if you're doing anything new. Don't let the possibility of being wrong keep you from standing up and trying.

☐ 9. **(Workaround)** Just make it a goal to know yourself completely without worrying about doing anything about your weaknesses. Ask everyone you respect. Do a 360° feedback assessment. Research has shown that just knowing about all of your weaknesses can actually lead to some improvement without actually working on them.

☐ 10. **(Workaround)** Similar to number 9, look at each critical weakness you identify and engage an internal or external person who is very good at that dimension to act in your behalf. Or delegate your weaknesses to your staff. Most of the time one or more on your staff will be better than you on several dimensions.

MORE HELP?

See *FYI For Your Improvement*™. We have coded each item to about 10 tips from the *FYI* book. To use this resource, the codes below refer to the chapter and then the tip number from the *FYI* book. For example, in item 17 below, 45-5 refers to Chapter 45—Personal Learning, tip 5. If you don't have a copy of *FYI*, it is available through Lominger at 952-345-3610 or www.lominger.com

17. Seeks feedback.
45-5; 55-1,3,4,6; 104-1; 106-4; 108-1,2,7

44. Is insightful about personal mistakes and failures; learns from them and moves on.
44-7; 57-1,5,10; 104-1; 108-1,2,3,4,7

71. Have seen this person substantially change based upon critical feedback, making a mistake, or learning something new.
44-7; 45-5; 54-1,10; 104-1; 106-4; 108-1,2,3,7

JOBS THAT WOULD ADD SKILLS IN THIS DIMENSION

☐ Out of Home Country Assignments—requiring conflicting cultures and a new and diverse population.

☐ Scope (very broad) Assignments—requiring communicating to a variety of people about a variety of topics.

☐ Cross Moves—requiring working with a new group of people from another function with a different background and viewpoint.

☐ Fix-its/Turnarounds—requiring helping people rapidly change what they are doing and building their skills to be more successful.

☐ Chair of Projects/Task Forces—requiring performing under tight deadlines and high visibility on an issue that matters to people higher up.

PART-TIME ASSIGNMENTS THAT WOULD ADD SKILLS IN THIS DIMENSION

☐ Make peace with an enemy or someone you've disappointed with a product or service or someone you've had some trouble with or don't get along well with.

☐ Assemble a team of diverse people to accomplish a difficult task.

☐ Handle a tough negotiation with an internal or external client or customer.

☐ Take on a tough and previously undoable project where others have tried but failed to come up with the right answer.

☐ Help shut down a plant, office, product line, business, operation, etc.

☐ Attend a self-awareness workshop that has 360° and live feed-back.

☐ Resolve a conflict between two people or two units.

☐ Integrate diverse systems, processes, or procedures across a decentralized or dispersed unit.

☐ Manage a dissatisfied internal or external customer; troubleshoot a performance or quality problem with a product or service.

☐ Lead a group through an unpopular change.

SUGGESTED READINGS

Bernstein, Albert J. and Sydney Craft Rozen. *Sacred bull: The inner obstacles that hold you back at work and how to overcome them*. New York: Wiley, 1994.

Bolton, Robert. *People skills: How to assert yourself, listen to others and resolve conflicts*. New York: Simon & Schuster, 1986.

Bolton, Robert and Dorothy Grover Bolton. *People styles at work*. New York: AMACOM, 1996.

Burley-Allen, Madelyn. *Listening: The forgotten skill*. New York: John Wiley & Sons, 1995.

Conger, Jay A. *Learning to lead*. San Francisco: Jossey-Bass, Inc., 1992.

DuBrin, Andrew J. *Your own worst enemy*. New York: AMACOM, 1992.

Holton, Bill and Cher Holton. *The manager's short course: Thirty-three tactics to upgrade your career*. New York: John Wiley & Sons, 1992.

Lombardo, Michael and Robert Eichinger. *The leadership machine*. Minneapolis: Lominger, 2002.

Prochaska, James O., John C. Norcross and Carlo C. DiClemente. *Changing for good*. New York: Avon Books, 1995.

Searing, Jill A. and Anne B. Lovett. *The career prescription: How to stop sabotaging your career and put it on a winning track*. Englewood Cliffs, NJ: Prentice Hall, 1995.

Stone, Florence M. and Randi T. Sachs. *The high-value manager —Developing the core competencies your organization needs*. New York: AMACOM, 1995.

17

17

DIMENSION 18
ROLE FLEXIBILITY

SKILLED

Behaves situationally; can move in many directions, play different roles, involve others or just act. Open to counter evidence.

UNSKILLED

May be seen as unbending; too much one-way—e.g., too participative or too directive.

ITEMS

☐ 18. Is able to play different roles and act differently depending upon the demands of the situation; behaves situationally rather than how he/she feels or would like to act.

☐ 45. Has a good balance between following due processes (respecting the rights and needs of others) and just acting to get things done.

☐ 72. After stating a position and being presented with reasonable counter evidence, can change his/her mind.

LEADERSHIP ARCHITECT® COMPETENCIES MOST ASSOCIATED WITH THIS DIMENSION

Strong

☐ 2. *Dealing with* Ambiguity

☐ 12. Conflict Management

☐ 40. *Dealing with* Paradox

☐ 45. Personal Learning

☐ 46. Perspective

Moderate

- ☐ 31. Interpersonal Savvy
- ☐ 33. Listening
- ☐ 53. *Drive for* Results

Light

- ☐ 16. *Timely* Decision Making
- ☐ 39. Organizing
- ☐ 51. Problem Solving
- ☐ 56. Sizing Up People

SOME CAUSES

- ☐ Always true to self
- ☐ Can't make smooth transitions
- ☐ Defensive
- ☐ Doesn't believe in playing multiple roles
- ☐ Doesn't read situations
- ☐ Doesn't shift roles easily or comfortably
- ☐ Not a good actor
- ☐ Not political
- ☐ One-trick pony
- ☐ Rigid and inflexible
- ☐ Single-tracked
- ☐ Stuck in the past

THE MAP

Complex jobs in complex organizations demand that we play different roles. There is nothing chameleon-like or disingenuous about this. You need to lead and follow, be tough and be yielding. One way of acting isn't sufficient. The person who can honestly and credibly play the most roles generally gets more done and wins.

SOME REMEDIES

☐ 1. It's all in a day's work: going from a tense meeting to a celebration for a notable accomplishment. Think of your day as a series of transitions. For a week, monitor your gear-shifting behavior at work and at home. What transitions give you the most trouble? The least? Why? Practice gear-shifting transitions. On the way between activities, think about the transition you're making and the frame of mind required to make it.

☐ 2. Work on acting in opposite ways. Deliver a tough message but do it in a compassionate way. Dig into the details while trying to establish the conceptual drivers as well. Take a strong stand but listen and leave room for others to shine.

☐ 3. Overdoing some of our strengths is typical. We push for results too hard; we analyze data too long; we try to be too nice. For our overdone behaviors, it's especially difficult to do the opposite. The key here is to balance what you do. If you're being too tough, stop and ask how the other person is doing. Ask yourself how you like to be treated. If you meddle, work on setting standards and outcomes. If you freeze under too much pressure, pause, take a drink of water, and ask yourself what is one productive thing you can do right now.

☐ 4. Interview people who are good at making transitions, such as fix-it managers, shut-down managers, or excellent parents. Talk with an actor or actress; get to know people who have recently joined your organization from places quite different. Talk to a therapist who hears a different problem every hour.

☐ 5. Recognize your triggers. Initial anxious responses last 45 to 60 seconds. They are marked by your characteristic emotional response. Learn to recognize your triggers: Voice go up? Shift in your chair? Harsh thoughts? Once you have figured out your triggers, ask why. Is it ego? Extra work? People you dislike or think are lazy? For each grouping, figure out what would be a more mature response. If it's too late, count to 10 or ask a clarifying question. Stall until the initial burst of glucose subsides.

☐ 6. Reduce conflict. Trade with the other side, find points of agreement, make sure to understand their point of view, be problem oriented. Don't try to win every battle. Focus on common-ground issues, and treat each conflict as one that needs to be resolved with fairness for both sides.

☐ 7. Think more outside in. What are the demands of this situation? Which of my approaches or styles will work best? Get out of your comfort zone of how you like to behave and consider the outside (customers, audience, person, group).

☐ 8. **(Workaround)** Engage internal or external people who can play the roles you can't and delegate the tasks to them.

☐ 9. **(Workaround)** Try to manage your schedule and time in single-role events. One meeting, one agenda. One event, one role requirement. One group, one thing to do. Put a little time or break between different situations.

☐ 10. **(Workaround)** Think of yourself as an actor playing a number of roles. An actor acts the role needed to make the play or movie work. Who they are is less important. Who they need to be is most important. Think about each key situation. How would Russell Crowe or Julia Roberts play the role? Body language? Voice? Pace? Process? Reactions? What are you trying to accomplish? What parts of you would work the best. See what works and what doesn't work. Maybe in time, you can actually become the parts you get good at.

MORE HELP?

See *FYI For Your Improvement*™. We have coded each item to about 10 tips from the *FYI* book. To use this resource, the codes below refer to the chapter and then the tip number from the *FYI* book. For example, in item 18 below, 40-1,2,3,5,6,7,9,10 refers to Chapter 40—*Dealing with* Paradox, tips 1,2,3,5,6,7,9 and 10. If you don't have a copy of *FYI*, it is available through Lominger at 952-345-3610 or www.lominger.com

18. Is able to play different roles and act differently depending upon the demands of the situation; behaves situationally rather than how he/she feels or would like to act.
40-1,2,3,5,6,7,9,10; 106-1,10

45. Has a good balance between following due processes (respecting the rights and needs of others) and just acting to get things done.
1-2,3; 23-2; 33-6; 36-3; 40-2,3,10; 64-8; 104-4

72. After stating a position and being presented with reasonable counter evidence, can change his/her mind.
12-1,5,7; 33-3; 37-1,2,4; 41-7; 104-4; 106-2

JOBS THAT WOULD ADD SKILLS IN THIS DIMENSION

☐ Out of Home Country Assignments—requiring conflicting cultures and a new and diverse population.

☐ Scope (very broad) Assignments—requiring communicating to a variety of people about a variety of topics.

☐ Chair of Projects/Task Forces—requiring performing under tight deadlines and high visibility on an issue that matters to people higher up.

☐ Fix-its/Turnarounds—requiring helping people rapidly change what they are doing and building their skills to be more successful.

☐ Cross Moves—requiring working with a new group of people from another function with a different background and viewpoint.

☐ Influencing Without Authority—working across organizational boundaries without the power to command attention where people and political skills are at a premium; conflict cannot be resolved with authority; influence is the main tool.

PART-TIME ASSIGNMENTS THAT WOULD ADD SKILLS IN THIS DIMENSION

☐ Assemble a team of diverse people to accomplish a difficult task.

☐ Take on a tough and previously undoable project where others have tried but failed to come up with the right answer.

☐ Lead a group through an unpopular change.

☐ Form a multifunctional team to tackle a common issue.

☐ Manage the renovation of an office, floor, building, warehouse, etc.

☐ Help shut down a plant, office, product line, business, operation, etc.

☐ Make peace with an enemy or someone you've disappointed with a product or service or someone you've had some trouble with or don't get along well with.

☐ Handle customer complaints and suggestions; troubleshoot a serious product or service breakdown.

☐ Represent the concerns of a group of nonexempt, clerical, administrative, or union employees to higher management to seek a resolution of a difficult issue.

☐ Take on a task or project you dislike or hate to do.

☐ Lobby for your organization on a contested issue in local, regional, state, federal, or an international government.

SUGGESTED READINGS

Bolton, Robert. *People skills: How to assert yourself, listen to others and resolve conflicts*. New York: Simon & Schuster, 1986.

Bolton, Robert and Dorothy Grover Bolton. *People styles at work*. New York: AMACOM, 1996.

Dimitrius, Jo-Ellan and Mark Mazzarella. *Reading people: How to understand people and predict their behavior— Anytime, anyplace*. New York: Random House, 1998.

Epstein, Seymour, Ph.D. with Archie Brodsky. *You're smarter than you think—How to develop your practical intelligence for success in living*. New York: Simon & Schuster, 1993.

Handy, Charles. *The age of paradox*. Boston: Harvard Business School Press, 1994.

Kheel, Theodore W. *The keys to conflict resolution—Proven methods of resolving disputes voluntarily*. New York: Four Walls Eight Windows, 1999.

Levine, Stewart. *Getting to resolution*. San Francisco: Berrett-Koehler Publishers, 1998.

Loehr, James E. *Stress for success*. New York: Times Business, 1997.

Nichols, Michael P. *The lost art of listening*. New York: The Guilford Press, 1995.

Van Slyke, Erik J. *Listening to conflict*. New York: AMACOM, 1999.

18

18

DIMENSION 19
SELF-AWARE

SKILLED

Candid, knows what he/she is good and lousy at, not afraid to admit it and compensate; may be seen as humble and human, but might also be seen as too revealing by some.

UNSKILLED

Neither knows strengths and weaknesses nor discloses much; may be enigmatic, badly perceive his/her skill set, rush in where he/she should stay out.

ITEMS

☐ 19. Understands his/her limits; compensates for what he/she isn't good at.

☐ 46. Candid to a fault about self, issues, and information (though not always with others who may be harmed).

☐ 73. Knows him/herself.

LEADERSHIP ARCHITECT® COMPETENCIES MOST ASSOCIATED WITH THIS DIMENSION

Strong

☐ 32. Learning on the Fly

☐ 44. Personal Disclosure

☐ 55. Self-Knowledge

Moderate

☐ 33. Listening

☐ 54. Self-Development

☐ 57. Standing Alone

Light

- [ ] 11. Composure
- [ ] 51. Problem Solving
- [ ] 56. Sizing Up People

SOME CAUSES

- [ ] Blames others for own faults
- [ ] Defensive
- [ ] Doesn't ask for feedback
- [ ] Doesn't care what others think
- [ ] Doesn't listen
- [ ] Doesn't read people well
- [ ] Excessively high self-appraisal
- [ ] Fear of discovery of weaknesses
- [ ] Not ambitious
- [ ] Not curious

THE MAP

People who don't know their strengths and weaknesses tend to overestimate themselves, a consistent finding in the research literature that has been related to both poor performance and being terminated. Knowing yourself helps you use your strengths better, compensate for what you're not good at, develop where you can, and avoid situations where you are unskilled. People who know themselves better do better.

SOME REMEDIES

- [ ] 1. Get more feedback. 360° feedback—where you compare your responses on a set of competencies to those of boss, peers, direct reports (if any), and sometimes customers—is the preferred approach. Many other avenues are open to you as well—boss,

128

confidantes, or a development partner if you're lucky enough to have one.

☐ 2. Focus on the highest and lowest ratings from each group. Don't spend time worrying about whether your scores are high or low in an absolute sense. 360° instruments aren't designed as performance assessments ordinarily. For development, you should worry about you relative to you. What are your highest and lowest ratings?

☐ 3. Ask why. Why am I seen this way? How did my strengths get to be so? Are my weaknesses things I avoid, am simply not skilled at, things I dislike or things I've never done? What experiences shaped my pattern? Do I have strengths that are related to my weaknesses, such as the smart person who makes others feel less so? Use this analysis to determine what is relatively easier and tougher for you to do.

☐ 4. Follow up. Prepare specific areas you are concerned about and ask people to respond in writing. Ask them what they would like to see you keep doing, start doing, stop doing, or do differently. If you know the people well, you can try face-to-face feedback, although you should know that this is usually blander and more positive than written feedback. If you do this, select specific areas and state what you think the issue or need for improvement is. Don't ask general questions. Get them to respond to your statements.

☐ 5. Seen as arrogant and/or defensive? Many people with a need in this area are seen as self-sufficient and disinterested in feedback and change. If this is the case, you may have to ask repeatedly. And regardless of the feedback, accept it. Don't say it's inaccurate or a one-time failing; don't argue or qualify. Just take it in. Use mental rehearsal to get ready for what may happen. If you comment at all, give examples of the behavior being described to validate what they are saying. Chances are good they are right. Defensive and arrogant people typically have major blind spots.

☐ 6. Even if the feedback is not true, you need to deal with it. If people, especially those above you, believe these things, your career will be damaged. You need to construct a plan to convince people of the untruth(s) by deeds, not words. Plan how you will act in critical situations and expect it to take quite a while for people to see you differently. It may take 10 times before people reconsider their view of you.

☐ 7. Disclose more. If you deny, minimize or excuse away mistakes and shortcomings, take a chance and admit that you're imperfect like everyone else. Let your inside thoughts out in the open more often. Sprinkle normal work conversation with doubts, what you're thinking about and what's getting in the way. Since you probably don't know how to do this, select three people who are good at admitting mistakes and shortcomings and observe how they do it.

☐ 8. You can compensate for your flat and downsides. All of us are poor at some things and beating on them is counterproductive. If you've failed or been lackluster in an area repeatedly, you can change jobs, restructure your job, or simply work to neutralize the downside.

☐ 9. The goal of self-awareness is full knowledge. What are my clear strengths and how can I use them better? What do I overdo? What are strengths I've been previously unaware of? What are known weaknesses? What are untested areas? And most important, what are my blind spots where I think or thought I was much better than others see me as being. It is blind spots above all else that stall careers.

☐ 10. **(Workaround)** Just make it a goal to know yourself completely without worrying about doing anything about your weaknesses. Ask everyone you respect. Do a 360° feedback assessment. Research has shown that just knowing about all of your weaknesses can actually lead to some improvement without actually working on them. Look at each critical weakness you identify and engage an internal or external person who is very good at that competency to act in your behalf. Or delegate your weaknesses to your staff. Most of the time one or more on your staff will be better than you on several competencies.

MORE HELP?

See *FYI For Your Improvement™*. We have coded each item to about 10 tips from the *FYI* book. To use this resource, the codes below refer to the chapter and then the tip number from the *FYI* book. For example, in item 19 below, 44-6,7 refers to Chapter 44—Personal Disclosure, tips 6 and 7. If you don't have a copy of *FYI,* it is available through Lominger at 952-345-3610 or www.lominger.com

19. Understands his/her limits; compensates for what he/she isn't good at.
44-6,7; 54-7; 55-1,3; 104-1,2; 108-1,4,7

46. Candid to a fault about self, issues, and information (though not always with others who may be harmed).
44-1,2,3,4,5,6,7,8,9,10

73. Knows him/herself.
55-1,2,3,4,5,6,7,8,9,10

JOBS THAT WOULD ADD SKILLS IN THIS DIMENSION

☐ Start-ups—requiring forging a new team and building new skills as you go.

☐ Out of Home Country Assignments—requiring conflicting cultures and a new and diverse population.

☐ Chair of Projects/Task Forces—requiring performing under tight deadlines and high visibility on an issue that matters to people higher up.

☐ Scope (very broad) Assignments—requiring communicating to a variety of new people about a variety of topics.

☐ Cross Moves—requiring working with a new group of people from another function with a different background and viewpoint.

☐ Influencing Without Authority—working across organizational boundaries without the power to command attention where people and political skills are at a premium; conflict cannot be resolved with authority; influence is the main tool.

PART-TIME ASSIGNMENTS THAT WOULD ADD SKILLS IN THIS DIMENSION

☐ Make peace with an enemy or someone you've disappointed with a product or service or someone you've had some trouble with or don't get along well with.

☐ Attend a self-awareness workshop that has 360° and live feedback.

☐ Take on a tough and previously undoable project where others have tried but failed to come up with the right answer.

☐ Assemble a team of diverse people to accomplish a difficult task.

☐ Handle customer complaints and suggestions.

☐ Help shut down a plant, office, product line, business, operation, etc.

☐ Try to learn something new, fun, or frivolous to see how good you can get (e.g., juggling, square dancing, magic).

☐ Work with a mentor and review all past assessments you have had and can remember, and summarize who you are and what that means for the rest of your career.

☐ Attend a course or an event which will push you beyond your usual limits and is outside your comfort zone (e.g., Outward Bound, language immersion training, sensitivity group, Toastmasters, clown school).

☐ Join a self-help or support group.

SUGGESTED READINGS

Bernstein, Albert J. and Sydney Craft Rozen. *Sacred bull: The inner obstacles that hold you back at work and how to overcome them.* New York: Wiley, 1994.

Bolton, Robert. *People skills: How to assert yourself, listen to others and resolve conflicts*. New York: Simon & Schuster, 1986.

Branden, Nathaniel. *The art of living consciously: The power of awareness to transform everyday life*. New York: Simon & Schuster, 1997.

Burley-Allen, Madelyn. *Listening: The forgotten skill*. New York: John Wiley & Sons, 1995.

Conger, Jay A. *Learning to lead*. San Francisco: Jossey-Bass, Inc., 1992.

DuBrin, Andrew J. *Your own worst enemy*. New York: AMACOM, 1992.

Holton, Bill and Cher Holton. *The manager's short course: Thirty-three tactics to upgrade your career*. New York: John Wiley & Sons, 1992.

Lombardo, Michael and Robert Eichinger. *The leadership machine*. Minneapolis: Lominger, 2002.

Prochaska, James O., John C. Norcross and Carlo C. DiClemente. *Changing for good*. New York: Avon Books, 1995.

Searing, Jill A. and Anne B. Lovett. *The career prescription: How to stop sabotaging your career and put it on a winning track*. Englewood Cliffs, NJ: Prentice Hall, 1995.

Stone, Florence M. and Randi T. Sachs. *The high-value manager —Developing the core competencies your organization needs*. New York: AMACOM, 1995.

19

19

HIGH

People high on this Factor like to tinker with ideas and put them into practice. They are likely to be highly interested in continuous improvements. They are cool under pressure, and can handle the heat and consequences of being in the vanguard of change efforts.

LOW

People low on this Factor may like things ordered and as usual. They may be uncomfortable with experimentation. Liking sameness, they may appear resistant or disinterested in innovation or the tinkering and conflict management required to make it work. At the extreme, they might be seen as perfectionists who try to get everything just so, thereby insulating themselves from criticism.

SOME CAUSES

- ☐ Avoids conflict
- ☐ Dislikes the noise of change
- ☐ Doesn't want to lead
- ☐ Fear of criticism
- ☐ Fear of failing in the new
- ☐ Fear of uncertainty
- ☐ Gets easily stressed and anxious
- ☐ Not curious
- ☐ Not experimental
- ☐ Perfectionist

continued

Factor III

- ☐ Prefers predictability
- ☐ Quiet, unchanging past
- ☐ Too comfortable
- ☐ Wed to the past

Factor III

DIMENSION 20
EXPERIMENTER

SKILLED

Likes test cases—ideas, products, services; fiddles with things to improve something or to come up with a creative solution; comfortable trying several times before finding the right solution.

UNSKILLED

Likes to have everything just so; may resist the new, criticizing its inevitable imperfections; may call experimentation sloppiness, and hold changes up to impossibly mature standards.

ITEMS

☐ 20. Is an inveterate tinkerer; can't leave things alone for long without seeking a new way.

☐ 47. Is creative and innovative.

☐ 74. Floats trial balloons, tries products and services not quite ready, serves up preliminary thinking, all in the service of a better final product.

LEADERSHIP ARCHITECT® COMPETENCIES MOST ASSOCIATED WITH THIS DIMENSION

Strong

☐ 2. *Dealing with* Ambiguity

☐ 14. Creativity

☐ 28. Innovation Management

☐ 32. Learning on the Fly

☐ 51. Problem Solving

20

Moderate

- ☐ 46. Perspective
- ☐ 61. Technical Learning

Light

- ☐ 1. Action Oriented
- ☐ 16. *Timely* Decision Making
- ☐ 40. *Dealing with* Paradox

SOME CAUSES

- ☐ Avoids conflict
- ☐ Can't think of anything new or different
- ☐ Comfortable with what is
- ☐ Defensive
- ☐ Doesn't like taking risks
- ☐ Doesn't like to be out front in the lead
- ☐ Fear of failure and making mistakes
- ☐ Impatient
- ☐ Not curious
- ☐ Perfectionist
- ☐ Slow
- ☐ Withdrawn and quiet

THE MAP

The more experiments, the more chances to learn to do something better. Too often we do things the same old way, yet expect a different outcome. Trial and error eventually leads to improvement. Most of the things we use today in life were not created instantly. Instead, they come along as the very last car in the long experimenting train.

SOME REMEDIES

☐ 1. Perfectionist? Learn to recognize it for what it is, collecting all the information to improve confidence and avoid criticism. Anyone with a brain and 100 percent of the information will make good decisions, but others are doing it with far less. When in the process of trying to solve something, try writing down what you would do at various points along the way. Then revisit it each time you gain more information. At what point would you have made the same decision as you did with all or more of the information? Most of the time, you could have settled upon a solution long before you actually did. Many of us wait an extra week or two, but our decision doesn't change.

☐ 2. Treat failures and mistakes as chances to learn. Successful executives report more failures and mistakes than do the less successful. You can't learn from things you're not doing. The key is to make small decisions, get instant feedback, correct, and get better. Getting it right the first time is not likely—be an incrementalist. Triple your learning opportunities by trying three small experiments.

☐ 3. Get away from your favorite solutions. They interfere with growth and change. Decide what you would most likely do, then don't do it. Carve out some time—talk with others, look for parallels in other organizations, talk to an expert in an unrelated field, pick some unusual or odd facts about the problem you're facing and see what they signal, brainstorm with a one-time problem solving group. Don't restrict your solution space.

☐ 4. Most innovations fail. The most successful innovators do it by sheer quantity and learning from failure. Edison took 3,000 shots at the lightbulb. Try lots of quick, low-impact experiments to increase the chances of success. For example, try five ways to test a product rather than one big carefully planned one. Look for something common in the failure that is never present when there is a success. Let the plan evolve from the tests.

☐ 5. Challenge the status quo. Creativity requires combining two things previously unconnected or changing how we look at them. It also requires generating ideas without judging them initially. People who do this well are atypical as well—they may be playful, contrary, and averse to many rules. You may have to buffer them somewhat and give them some room. You won't get anything new by following the normal set-a-goal-and-time-schedule approach.

☐ 6. Up your risk comfort by letting others experiment. Delegate more; pick some small things you do right. Pick an easy piece of a larger project, then pick a couple of tougher pieces. Review each one to see what went well and not well.

☐ 7. Lack boldness? Tired of what you do? Find something that needs doing for which you have some enthusiasm. Appoint yourself as champion. Throw out trial balloons to see if your notion spurs some interest. Find an experimenter to go in with you. Bring in a heavy expert. Plant seeds at every opportunity.

☐ 8. **(Workaround)** While not interested or willing to be creative and innovative yourself, give others around you the freedom to run. Delegate experimentation. Don't resist. Don't be a critic. Don't get in the way.

☐ 9. **(Workaround)** Engage internal and external resources who are creative, innovative, and who like to experiment. Let them identify the most likely areas for the new and different.

☐ 10. **(Workaround)** Get help if you are a change manager. Use an internal or external consultant who specializes in planning for and managing change. Or delegate it to your staff. Let them plan for and manage the change.

MORE HELP?

See *FYI For Your Improvement*™. We have coded each item to about 10 tips from the *FYI* book. To use this resource, the codes below refer to the chapter and then the tip number from the *FYI* book. For example, in item 20 below, 1-3,5 refers to Chapter 1—Action Oriented, tips 3 and 5. If you don't have a copy of *FYI*, it is available through Lominger at 952-345-3610 or www.lominger.com

20. Is an inveterate tinkerer; can't leave things alone for long without seeking a new way.
1-3,5; 2-1,3,6; 14-1,4; 32-4,9; 51-2

47. Is creative and innovative.
14-1,2,3,4,5,9,10; 28-2,3,4

74. Floats trial balloons, tries products and services not quite ready, serves up preliminary thinking, all in the service of a better final product.
1-3; 2-1,2,7; 16-7; 32-3,4,9; 57-1,9

JOBS THAT WOULD ADD SKILLS IN THIS DIMENSION

☐ Fix-its/Turnarounds—requiring making tough decisions impacting a variety of people and constituencies and trying a lot of new things.

☐ Start-ups—requiring forging a new team and trying a variety of new and first-time initiatives on a tight timetable.

☐ Crisis or Change Manager—requiring resourceful decisions under tight time pressure with a low level of consultation.

☐ Scope (very broad) Assignments—requiring a variety of initiatives about a variety of topics in areas new to the person.

☐ Out of Home Country Assignments—requiring communicating to a new and diverse population and taking first-time actions in a new environment.

20

PART-TIME ASSIGNMENTS THAT WOULD ADD SKILLS IN THIS DIMENSION

☐ Relaunch an existing product or service that's not doing well by trying things not tried before.

☐ Assemble a team of diverse people to accomplish a difficult task.

☐ Manage a group of people working on a fix-it or turnaround situation or project.

☐ Take on a tough and undoable project, one where others who have tried it have failed.

☐ Launch a new product, service, or process.

☐ Build a multifunctional project team to tackle a common business issue or problem.

☐ Plan a new site for a building (plant, field office, headquarters, etc.).

☐ Handle a tough negotiation with an internal or external client or customer.

☐ Take on a task you dislike or hate to do.

☐ Work on a team that has to integrate diverse systems (move from using five computer platforms into one), processes (moving from ISO, TQM, and Six Sigma into only one of the three), or procedures (five competency models into one) across decentralized and/or dispersed units where you have to find the most common solution.

SUGGESTED READINGS

De Bono, Edward. *Serious creativity: Using the power of lateral thinking to create new ideas*. New York: HarperBusiness, 1992.

Drucker, Peter F. *Innovation and entrepreneurship*. New York: Harper & Row, 1985.

Drucker, Peter F. *Innovation and entrepreneurship: Practice and principles* [sound recording]. New York: AMACOM; Albuquerque, NM: Distributed by Newman, 1985.

Firestine, Roger L., Ph.D. *Leading on the creative edge—Gaining competitive advantage through the power of creative problem solving*. Colorado Springs, CO: Piñon Press, 1996.

Futurist Magazine. http://www.wfs.org

Hamel, G. *Leading the revolution*. Boston: Harvard Business School Press, 2000.

Hamel, Gary and C.K. Prahalad. *Competing for the future*. Boston: Harvard Business School Press, 1994.

Hammer, Michael and James A. Champy. *Reengineering the corporation: A manifesto for business revolution*. New York: HarperBusiness, 2001.

Kanter, Rosabeth Moss, John Kao and Fred Wiersema (Editors). *Innovation: Breakthrough thinking at 3M, DuPont, GE, Pfizer and Rubbermaid*. New York: HarperBusiness, 1997.

Kidder, Tracy. *The soul of a new machine*. Boston: Little, Brown, 1981.

Kotter, John P. *Leading change*. Boston: Harvard Business School Press, 1996.

Kotter, John P. and Dan S. Cohen. *The heart of change: Real-life stories of how people change their organizations*. Watertown, MA: Harvard Business School Press, 2002.

Peters, Tom. *Liberation management*. New York: Knopf, 1992.

Peters, Tom. *Liberation management* [sound recording]. New York: Random House Audio, 1992.

Robert, Michel. *Product innovation strategy*. New York: McGraw-Hill, Inc., 1995.

20

20

DIMENSION 21
INNOVATION MANAGER

SKILLED

Can manage ideas so they become practice; can move ideas to market; is both team and organizationally savvy.

UNSKILLED

Has problems with implementing ideas; may have trouble with the process of innovation, getting ideas to fruition in a team, or getting things done in an organizational setting.

ITEMS

- ☐ 21. Can manage a team from idea to implementation.
- ☐ 48. Can personally take an innovative idea and move it all the way to practice.
- ☐ 75. Knows how to get things done outside of formal channels as well as within them; is savvy about who to go to, and when.

LEADERSHIP ARCHITECT® COMPETENCIES MOST ASSOCIATED WITH THIS DIMENSION

Strong

- ☐ 28. Innovation Management
- ☐ 38. Organizational Agility
- ☐ 39. Organizing
- ☐ 52. Process Management

Moderate

- ☐ 36. Motivating Others
- ☐ 37. Negotiating

21

Light

- [ ] 2. *Dealing with* Ambiguity
- [ ] 12. Conflict Management
- [ ] 20. Directing Others
- [ ] 47. Planning
- [ ] 51. Problem Solving

SOME CAUSES

- [ ] A loner
- [ ] Avoids conflict
- [ ] Dislikes risk
- [ ] Doesn't like to be out front leading
- [ ] Impatient
- [ ] Likes to be right
- [ ] Not creative
- [ ] Not inspiring
- [ ] Not politically savvy
- [ ] Not resourceful
- [ ] Not well networked
- [ ] Not well organized
- [ ] Shy and withdrawn
- [ ] Too comfortable with what is

THE MAP

Thinking through and managing innovation is different from ordinary planning and execution. It requires understanding the creative process and the high failure rates associated with innovation. Growth and progress ride on the back of innovation. Being able to find and then implement the new, different, and the unique drives progress.

SOME REMEDIES

☐ 1. Understand your markets. What have your customers done in the past? What have your competitors been successful with? Which new products or services failed and which succeeded? Why? Talk to the strategic planners in your organization. Access experts. Talk to key customers. Consult your team.

☐ 2. Most innovations fail. The most successful innovators do it by sheer quantity and learning from failure. Edison took 3,000 shots at the lightbulb. Try lots of quick, inexpensive experiments to increase the chances of success. For example, try five ways to test a product rather than one big carefully planned one. Look for something common in the failure that is never present when there is a success. Let the plan evolve from the tests.

☐ 3. Treat failures and mistakes as chances to learn. Successful executives report more failures and mistakes than do the less successful. You can't learn from things you're not doing. The key is to make small decisions, get instant feedback, correct, and get better. Getting it right the first time is not likely—be an incrementalist. Triple your learning opportunities by trying three small experiments.

☐ 4. Challenge the status quo. Creativity requires combining two things previously unconnected or changing how we look at them. It also requires generating ideas without judging them initially. People who do this well are atypical as well—they may be playful, contrary, and averse to many rules. You may have to buffer them somewhat and give them some room. You won't get anything new by following the normal set-a-goal-and-time-schedule approach.

☐ 5. Getting creativity out of a group. Solutions typically outweigh questions eight to one in problem solving meetings. Have the group ask more questions and spend half its time really looking at a problem statement. Have the group take a product/service you are dissatisfied with and represent it visually—flowchart it or use a series of pictures. Cut it up into its component pieces and

147

reorder them. Ask how you could combine three pieces into one. Look for patterns. Pull in fresh thinking into the group (use customers, people who know nothing about the area). Many studies have shown that the more diverse the group, the fresher the thinking. Creativity starts with lots of ideas and thorough examination of the problem.

☐ 6. Innovation is often like an orphan in an organization. Early in the process, resources will probably be tight. You will have to deal with other units and detractors. Be prepared to state the value again and again. What problem will it solve? How can it help the organization or other units? Think carefully about whom to go to and how to gain support. Appeal to the common good, trade something, and work to minimize negative effects on others. Work from the outside in. Determine the demands and interests of groups and individuals and appeal to those.

☐ 7. Give up too soon on an idea? If you have trouble going back the second or third time, then switch approaches. For example, you could meet with all stakeholders, a single key stakeholder, present the idea to a group, call in an expert to buttress your innovation, or project various scenarios showing the value of the idea.

☐ 8. Inspire your team. Innovation is tougher than work as usual. Celebrate wins, measure progress in small steps, have members of the groups present promising results, establish common cause, reinforce often why this is important, set small checkpoints and little goals, and treat failures as exciting chances to learn how to do it better.

☐ 9. **(Workaround)** Acknowledge that you are not the best at it and delegate it to your staff to plan and do. Give them room to run. Be sure to look for innovators when adding people to your team.

☐ 10. **(Workaround)** Engage internal or external experts in managing innovation. Let them plan and help you execute.

MORE HELP?

See *FYI For Your Improvement*™. We have coded each item to about 10 tips from the *FYI* book. To use this resource, the codes below refer to the chapter and then the tip number from the *FYI* book. For example, in item 21 below, 28-1,2,3,4,6,7,8,9,10 refers to Chapter 28—Innovation Management, tips 1,2,3,4,6,7,8,9 and 10. If you don't have a copy of *FYI*, it is available through Lominger at 952-345-3610 or www.lominger.com

21. Can manage a team from idea to implementation.
28-1,2,3,4,6,7,8,9,10; 60-1

48. Can personally take an innovative idea and move it all the way to practice.
28-1,7,8,9,10; 43-1; 57-1,3,7,9

75. Knows how to get things done outside of formal channels as well as within them; is savvy about who to go to, and when.
38-4,8,9,10; 42-1,5; 48-2,3,9; 64-8

JOBS THAT WOULD ADD SKILLS IN THIS DIMENSION

☐ Start-ups—requiring forging a new team and trying things for the first time on a tight timetable.

☐ Fix-its/Turnarounds—requiring trying new things to change the situation around where others have failed.

☐ Scope (very broad) Assignments—requiring working on a variety of initiatives across diverse areas.

☐ Chair of Projects/Task Forces—requiring finding new and effective solutions under tight deadlines and high visibility on an issue that matters to people higher up.

☐ Line to Staff Switches—requiring addressing a new group of people with different functional homes and a different viewpoint on the world with new and different solutions.

21

PART-TIME ASSIGNMENTS THAT WOULD ADD SKILLS IN THIS DIMENSION

☐ Relaunch an existing product or service that's not doing well.

☐ Manage a group of people involved in tackling a fix-it or turn-around project.

☐ Integrate diverse systems, processes, or procedures across decentralized and/or dispersed units.

☐ Build a multifunctional project team to tackle a common business issue or problem.

☐ Launch a new product, service, or process.

☐ Manage a group of people in a rapidly expanding operation.

☐ Take on a tough and undoable project, one where others who have tried it have failed.

☐ Manage a group through a significant business crisis.

☐ Plan for and start up something small (secretarial pool, athletic program, suggestion system, program, etc.).

☐ Plan an off-site meeting, conference, convention, trade show event, etc.

SUGGESTED READINGS

Bolton, Robert and Dorothy Grover Bolton. *People styles at work*. New York: AMACOM, 1996.

Bossidy, Larry, Ram Charan and Charles Burck (Contributor). *Execution: The discipline of getting things done*. New York: Crown Business Publishing, 2002.

Carr, David K. and Henry J. Johansson. *Best practices in reengineering*. New York: McGraw-Hill, Inc., 1995.

Drucker, Peter F. *Innovation and entrepreneurship*. New York: Harper & Row, 1985.

Drucker, Peter F. *Innovation and entrepreneurship: Practice and principles* [sound recording]. New York: AMACOM; Albuquerque, NM: Distributed by Newman, 1985.

Futurist Magazine. http://www.wfs.org

Hamel, G. *Leading the revolution*. Boston: Harvard Business School Press, 2000.

Hamel, Gary and C.K. Prahalad. *Competing for the future*. Boston: Harvard Business School Press, 1994.

Hammer, Michael and James A. Champy. *Reengineering the corporation: A manifesto for business revolution*. New York: HarperBusiness, 2001.

Kanter, Rosabeth Moss, John Kao, and Fred Wiersema (Editors). *Innovation: Breakthrough thinking at 3M, DuPont, GE, Pfizer and Rubbermaid*. New York: HarperBusiness, 1997.

Keen, Peter G.W. *The process edge—Creating value where it counts*. Boston: Harvard Business School Press, 1998.

Kidder, Tracy. *The soul of a new machine*. Boston: Little, Brown, 1981.

Koch, Richard. *The 80/20 principle: The secret of achieving more with less*. New York: Currency/Doubleday, 1998.

Kotter, John P. *Leading change*. Boston: Harvard Business School Press, 1996.

Kotter, John P. and Dan S. Cohen. *The heart of change: Real-life stories of how people change their organizations*. Watertown, MA: Harvard Business School Press, 2002.

Moskowitz, Robert. *How to organize your work and your life*. New York: Doubleday, 1993.

Peters, Tom. *Liberation management*. New York: Knopf, 1992.

Peters, Tom. *Liberation management* [sound recording]. New York: Random House Audio, 1992.

Robert, Michel. *Product innovation strategy*. New York: McGraw-Hill, Inc., 1995.

The Systems Thinker®. Waltham, MA: Pegasus Communications, Inc., 781-398-9700.

21

21

DIMENSION 22
TAKING THE HEAT

SKILLED

Philosophical about personal attacks; knows that people will be upset by change, negative consequences are possible; goes ahead with change.

UNSKILLED

May fold up under pressure or in the face of being in trouble with people; may try too hard to please everyone; may simply avoid such situations.

ITEMS

☐ 22. Knows that change is unsettling; can take a lot of heat, even when it gets personal.

☐ 49. Doesn't let others' reactions to his/her mistakes and failures be a deterrent to going ahead if he/she thinks something will eventually work.

☐ 76. Lives with negative consequences of being ahead of others on change.

LEADERSHIP ARCHITECT® COMPETENCIES MOST ASSOCIATED WITH THIS DIMENSION

Strong

☐ 2. *Dealing with* Ambiguity

☐ 11. Composure

☐ 12. Conflict Management

☐ 57. Standing Alone

22

Moderate

- ☐   9. Command Skills
- ☐ 41. Patience
- ☐ 43. Perseverance
- ☐ 65. *Managing* Vision and Purpose

Light

- ☐ 26. Humor
- ☐ 33. Listening
- ☐ 34. Managerial Courage
- ☐ 37. Negotiating
- ☐ 40. *Dealing with* Paradox

SOME CAUSES

- ☐ Avoids conflict
- ☐ Avoids criticism
- ☐ Cares a lot about what people think
- ☐ Comfortable with the way things are
- ☐ Defensive
- ☐ Doesn't like to be first
- ☐ Doesn't listen
- ☐ Gets easily upset
- ☐ Impatient with others not up-to-speed
- ☐ Not well networked
- ☐ Perfectionist
- ☐ Prefers to share responsibility
- ☐ Stops if there is resistance
- ☐ Takes criticism personally

22

THE MAP

To be a change champion, you have to be ready to pull some arrows out of various places, including your back. Change is scary, frustrating, and anxiety-producing for many. One reaction is to attack the change agent directly or, more likely, indirectly. Sabotage is common. All of this is natural. We are comfort-zone, nest-building organisms. We like things to stay the same. Those who try to mess with our comfort zone will feel our wrath. Successful change agents know this and absorb and chill unproductive noise by continuing to move forward.

SOME REMEDIES

☐ 1. Leading is risky. You have to defend what you're doing, so convince yourself first that you are on the right track. Be prepared to explain again and again. Lightning bolts from detractors, people unsettled by change, and people who will always say it could have been done differently, better, and cheaper. To prepare for this, think about the 10 objections that will come up and mentally rehearse how you will reply. Listen patiently to people's concerns, acknowledge them, then explain why you think the change will be beneficial. Attack positions, but not people.

☐ 2. Recognize your triggers. Initial anxious responses last 45 to 60 seconds. They are marked by your characteristic emotional response. Learn to recognize your triggers: Voice go up? Shift in your chair? Harsh thoughts? Once you have figured out your triggers, ask why. Is it ego? Extra work? People you dislike or think are lazy? For each grouping, figure out what would be a more mature response. If it's too late, count to 10 or ask a clarifying question. Stall until the initial burst of glucose and adrenaline subsides.

☐ 3. Expect trouble and admit that 20 to 50 percent of the time will be spent debugging, fixing mistakes, and figuring out what went wrong. Treat each one as a chance to learn. It's a work in progress.

22

☐ 4. How changes should be made should be as open as possible. Your job is the what and the why. Studies show that people work harder when they have a sense of choice over how they accomplish the new and different.

☐ 5. Keep conflicts small. Find out what the points of agreement are rather than focusing on the disagreements only. Don't resort to general statements such as "We have trust problems with your unit." Keep the concern specific—stick to whats and whens.

☐ 6. What if you're attacked? Let the other side vent, but don't react directly or instantly. Pause. Listen. Nod. Ask clarifying questions. Ask open-ended questions like "What could I do to help?" Restate their position so they know you've heard them. You don't have to do anything to appease, just listen and accept that they are irritated. Your goal is to calm the situation so you can get back to more reasonable discussion.

☐ 7. Lack boldness? Tired of what you do? Find something that needs changing for which you have some enthusiasm. Appoint yourself as the change champion. Throw out trial balloons to see if your notion spurs some interest. Find an experimenter to go in with you. Bring in a heavy expert. Plant seeds at every opportunity.

☐ 8. Give up too soon on an idea? If you have trouble going back the second or third time, then switch approaches. For example, you could meet with all stakeholders, a single key stakeholder, present the idea to a group, call in an expert to buttress your innovation, or project various scenarios showing the value of the idea.

☐ 9. The end game. Sometimes, try as you might, nothing works. The detractors are recalcitrant. Then, rarely, you may have to pull someone aside and say, "I've heard all your worries and have tried to respond to them. Now I'm moving on. Are you on or off the train?"

☐ 10. **(Workaround)** Share the heat. If it's just not in your nature to take the heat of leading change, use a participative strategy.

Spread it so if there is heat, everyone gets just a bit warm. Get the affected people together to scope out the need, plan for and execute the change. You will give up some control and things may not be done exactly as you would like.

MORE HELP?

See *FYI For Your Improvement*™. We have coded each item to about 10 tips from the *FYI* book. To use this resource, the codes below refer to the chapter and then the tip number from the *FYI* book. For example, in item 22 below, 2-1 refers to Chapter 2—*Dealing with Ambiguity*, tip 1. If you don't have a copy of *FYI*, it is available through Lominger at 952-345-3610 or www.lominger.com

22. Knows that change is unsettling; can take a lot of heat, even when it gets personal.
2-1; 12-3,4; 57-1,2,4,6,7; 65-3,7

49. Doesn't let others' reactions to his/her mistakes and failures be a deterrent to going ahead if he/she thinks something will eventually work.
12-3,4; 57-1,2,3,5,6,7,8,9

76. Lives with negative consequences of being ahead of others on change.
2-1; 12-3,4; 57-1,4,5,6,7; 65-3,7

JOBS THAT WOULD ADD SKILLS IN THIS DIMENSION

☐ Crisis or Change Manager—requiring tough-minded decisions under tight time pressure with a low level of consultation and high visibility.

☐ Out of Home Country Assignments—requiring communicating to a new and diverse population and making decisions and taking actions with less direct support and supervision.

☐ Start-ups—requiring forging a new team and acting on a variety of new and first-time subjects on a tight timetable with little precedence.

22

- Influencing Without Authority—acting across organizational boundaries without the power to command attention and compliance.

- Fix-its/Turnarounds—requiring making tough decision impacting a variety of people and constituencies under high visibility.

PART-TIME ASSIGNMENTS THAT WOULD ADD SKILLS IN THIS DIMENSION

- Manage a group of balky and resisting people through an unpopular change or project.

- Take on a tough and undoable project, one where others who have tried it have failed.

- Manage a group of people involved in tackling a fix-it or turn-around project.

- Help shut down a plant, regional office, product line, business, operation, etc.

- Handle a tough negotiation with an internal or external client or customer, or manage a dissatisfied internal or external customer; troubleshoot a performance or quality problem with a product or service.

- Resolve an issue in conflict between two people, units, geographies, functions, etc.

- Make peace with an enemy or someone you've disappointed with a product or service or someone you've had some trouble with or don't get along well with.

- Manage a group through a significant business crisis.

- Manage a cost-cutting project where the cuts are deep.

- Plan a new site for a building (plant, field office, headquarters, etc.).

☐ Work on a team that has to integrate diverse systems (move from using five computer platforms into one), processes (moving from ISO, TQM, and Six Sigma into only one of the three), or procedures (five competency models into one) across decentralized and/or dispersed units where you have to find the most common solution.

☐ Plan a first-time off-site meeting, conference, convention, trade show, event, etc.

☐ Prepare and present a proposal of some consequence to top management.

☐ Manage the renovation of an office, floor, building, meeting room, warehouse, etc.

☐ Work on a team that's deciding who to keep and who to let go in a layoff, shutdown, delayering, or divestiture.

☐ Be a member of a union-negotiating or grievance-handling team.

☐ Be a change agent; create a symbol for change; lead the rallying cry; champion a significant change and implementation.

SUGGESTED READINGS

Bernstein, Albert J. and Sydney Craft Rozen. *Sacred bull: The inner obstacles that hold you back at work and how to overcome them*. New York: Wiley, 1994.

Bolton, Robert. *People skills: How to assert yourself, listen to others and resolve conflicts*. New York: Simon & Schuster, 1986.

Caponigro, Jeffrey R. *The crisis counselor: The executive's guide to avoiding, managing, and thriving on crises that occur in all businesses*. Southfield, MI: Barker Business Books, Inc., 1998.

Cox, Danny and John Hoover. *Leadership when the heat's on*. New York: McGraw-Hill, Inc., 1992.

22

Dimitrius, Jo-Ellan and Mark Mazzarella. *Reading people: How to understand people and predict their behavior—Anytime, anyplace.* New York: Random House, 1998.

DuBrin, Andrew J. *Your own worst enemy.* New York: AMACOM, 1992.

Kheel, Theodore W. *The keys to conflict resolution—Proven methods of resolving disputes voluntarily.* New York: Four Walls Eight Windows, 1999.

Lee, John H. with Bill Stott. *Facing the fire: Experiencing and expressing anger appropriately.* New York: Bantam Books, 1993.

Levine, Stewart. *Getting to resolution.* San Francisco: Berrett-Koehler Publishers, 1998.

Loehr, James E. *Stress for success.* New York: Times Business, 1997.

Meyers, Gerald C. with John Holusha. *When it hits the fan: Managing the nine crises of business.* Boston: Houghton Mifflin, 1986.

Neuhauser, Peg. *Tribal warfare in organizations.* New York: Harper & Row, 1988.

Van Slyke, Erik J. *Listening to conflict.* New York: AMACOM, 1999.

22

DIMENSION 23
VISIONING

SKILLED

Introduces a different slant; good at "what ifs" and scenarios.

UNSKILLED

Doesn't come up with new or many wrinkles to the old; may have trouble seeing fresh scenarios or where they might lead.

ITEMS

- ☐ 23. Asks "Why can't it be done?"
- ☐ 50. Introduces a different slant into almost any discussion.
- ☐ 77. Good at envisioning and playing "what if" games and exercises; good at generating multiple scenarios.

LEADERSHIP ARCHITECT® COMPETENCIES MOST ASSOCIATED WITH THIS DIMENSION

Strong

- ☐ 2. *Dealing with* Ambiguity
- ☐ 14. Creativity
- ☐ 46. Perspective
- ☐ 51. Problem Solving

Moderate

- ☐ 12. Conflict Management
- ☐ 57. Standing Alone
- ☐ 58. Strategic Agility
- ☐ 65. *Managing* Vision and Purpose

23

Light

☐ 28. Innovation Management

☐ 30. Intellectual Horsepower

☐ 32. Learning on the Fly

SOME CAUSES

☐ Avoids risks

☐ Defensive

☐ Doesn't like being first or out front of others

☐ Doesn't like to speculate

☐ Fear of rejection of ideas

☐ Narrow background

☐ Not creative

☐ Not curious

☐ Prefers past solutions

☐ Prefers to stick with what is known

☐ Shy and withdrawn

☐ Single-tracked

☐ Too comfortable with what is

THE MAP

Visioning is an acquired skill, a combination of accessing history and trends and thinking ahead. How successful could you be if you knew all of the scores of future athletic contests? What if you knew the outcome of future professional fights? The winner of the World Series? Which stocks will go up in the market? What about the next trend in your business? The next market or country to latch on to your product or service? The next way to organize companies to be more productive? The next big thing in your product line? Visioning opens the door to the future and increases your chances of acting on target when the future gets here. The best way to prepare for an event is to know about it ahead of time. An even better path is to create the future you want.

SOME REMEDIES

☐ 1. Futuring is a series of educated "what ifs." To make more informed guesses, read periodicals with a global perspective, such as the *New York Times*, the *Economist*, *International Herald Tribune*, *BusinessWeek*, *Forbes*, *Futurist* and the *Atlantic Monthly*. These periodicals do an excellent job of setting historical context as well as explaining how things got to be the way they are. The more you know about past and present trends, the better your "what ifs" will become.

☐ 2. Learn more about your business. Talk to the people who know. Meet with the strategic planners, and read every significant document you can find about your business, it's customers and competitors. Reduce your understanding to rules of thumb and use these to image what initiative could make a huge difference.

☐ 3. Work on your visual side. Learn storyboarding, a pictorial technique of representing a problem or process. Use mindmapping, a wonderfully branching way to plan, examine ideas, and simply think differently. Get some scenario training, then implement it with your team to come up with likely futures. Use flowcharting software packages. Close your eyes and see what the outcome would look like. Come up with an image or symbol that embodies the vision. People are much more likely to get excited by stories, symbols, and images than a white paper explaining the plan.

☐ 4. Make your mind a bit sillier. You don't have to tell anyone what you're doing. Ask what song is this problem like? Find an analogy to your problem in nature, in children's toys, in anything that has a physical structure.

☐ 5. Look for anomalies, unusual facts that don't quite fit in. Why did sales go down when they should have gone up? It could be

23

random, but maybe not. Look for patterns, something present in failures but not present in successes. Even more useful, look for elements present in successes but never present in a failure. This will yield some insight into underlying principles.

☐ 6. Hunt for parallels in other organizations and in remote areas totally outside your field. By this, we don't mean best practices, which come and go. Find a parallel situation to the underlying issue—for example, who has to do things really fast (Domino's, FedEx)? Who has to deal with maximum ambiguity (emergency room, a newspaper, police dispatchers)?

☐ 7. Hunt for parallels in history. There are always plenty of candidates. Harry Truman used the National Archives to form a "Council of Presidents" to see what others had done in parallel situations.

☐ 8. Convene a group with the widest possible variety of backgrounds. (Yes, we mean widest. It makes no difference if they know anything about the problem.) During World War II it was discovered that groups with maximum diversity produced the most creative solutions to problems. You're looking for fresh approaches here, not practicality. That comes later as you sift through the ideas.

☐ 9. **(Workaround)** Leave the visioning to others. Hire an expert. Acknowledge its importance and get out of the way. Don't reject ideas too soon. Let them simmer. If you do reject, provide the why. Give them time and resources. Let the creative juices flow. Don't criticize. Don't require outcomes too soon. If you have given up on becoming a visionary, you have to be patient with others and give them leeway and time.

☐ 10. **(Workaround)** Share the visioning task with your team. Get everyone visioning. Be the ringmaster. Let the visions flow without evaluation at first. Then, test them for credibility. Narrow them down to the few most likely possibilities. Then draw up an action plan for each of them.

MORE HELP?

See *FYI For Your Improvement*™. We have coded each item to about 10 tips from the *FYI* book. To use this resource, the codes below refer to the chapter and then the tip number from the *FYI* book. For example, in item 23 below, 32-1,2,3,4 refers to Chapter 32—Learning on the Fly, tips 1,2,3 and 4. If you don't have a copy of *FYI*, it is available through Lominger at 952-345-3610 or www.lominger.com

23. Asks "Why can't it be done?"
    32-1,2,3,4; 51-4; 57-1,3,5,7,8

50. Introduces a different slant into almost any discussion.
    14-1,3,4,5; 32-1,2,3; 46-1; 58-3,9

77. Good at envisioning and playing "what if" games and exercises; good at generating multiple scenarios.
    5-6; 14-1,2; 46-1,2,3; 58-3,4,6; 65-9

JOBS THAT WOULD ADD SKILLS IN THIS DIMENSION

☐ Heavy Strategic Demands—requiring significant strategic thinking and planning which charts new ground, along with selling the vision to a critical audience.

☐ Scope (very broad) Assignments—requiring strategizing on a number of different fronts while tying it all into a single trust and vision message.

☐ Start-ups—requiring creating a from-the-ground-up strategy and vision to motivate new people on a tight timetable.

☐ Out of Home Country Assignments—requiring strategizing in a new environment and communicating the vision to new and different people.

☐ Fix-its/Turnarounds—requiring making tough strategic and tactical decisions impacting a variety of people and constituencies and communicating the vision clearly and quickly.

23

PART-TIME ASSIGNMENTS THAT WOULD ADD SKILLS IN THIS DIMENSION

☐ Relaunch an existing product or service that's not doing well, requiring a new vision.

☐ Launch a new product, service, or process.

☐ Take on a tough and undoable project, one where others who have tried it have failed where a new approach is needed.

☐ Manage an ad hoc, temporary group of people involved in tackling a fix-it or turnaround project where a new solution is called for.

☐ Prepare and present a strategic proposal of some consequence to top management which involves a change in direction.

☐ Build a multifunctional project team to tackle a common business issue or problem.

☐ Work on a team that has to integrate diverse systems (move from using five computer platforms into one), processes (moving from ISO, TQM, and Six Sigma into only one of the three), or procedures (five competency models into one) across decentralized and/or dispersed units where you have to find the most common solution.

☐ Work on a project that involves travel and study of an issue, acquisition, or joint venture off-shore or overseas, with a report back to management.

☐ Manage a group through a significant business crisis.

☐ Seek out and use a seed budget to create and pursue a personal idea, product, or service.

SUGGESTED READINGS

Atlantic Monthly. http://www.theatlantic.com

Belasco, James A. and Jerre Stead. *Soaring with the Phoenix—Renewing the vision, reviving the spirit, and re-creating the success of your company*. New York: Warner Books, 1999.

BusinessWeek. http://www.businessweek.com

Champy, James and Nitin Nohria. *The arc of ambition*. Cambridge, MA: Perseus Publishing, 2001.

Collins, J. *Good to great*. New York: Harper Collins, 2001.

Commentary Magazine. http://www.commentarymagazine.com

De Bono, Edward. *Six thinking hats*. Boston: Little, Brown, 1985.

Drucker, P. (1999). *Management challenges for the 21st century*. New York: HarperBusiness.

Dudik, E. *Strategic renaissance*. New York: AMACOM, 2000.

Economist. http://www.economist.com

Futurist Magazine. http://www.wfs.org

Hale, Guy. *The leader's edge—Mastering the five skills of breakthrough thinking*. Burr Ridge, IL: Irwin Professional Publishing, 1996.

Hamel, G. *Leading the revolution*. Boston: Harvard Business School Press, 2000.

Hamel, Gary and C.K. Prahalad. *Competing for the future*. Boston, MA: Harvard Business School Press, 1994.

International Herald Tribune. http://www.iht.com

Kanter, Rosabeth Moss, John Kao and Fred Wiersema (Editors). *Innovation: Breakthrough thinking at 3M, DuPont, GE, Pfizer and Rubbermaid*. New York: HarperBusiness, 1997.

Kennedy, Paul M. *The rise and fall of the great powers: Economic change and military conflict from 1500 to 2000*. New York: Random House, 1987.

23

Kotter, John P. *Leading change*. Boston: Harvard Business School Press, 1996.

Kotter, John P. and Dan S. Cohen. *The heart of change: Real-life stories of how people change their organizations*. Watertown, MA: Harvard Business School Press, 2002.

Nadler, Gerald, Ph.D. and Shozo Hibino, Ph.D. *Breakthrough thinking—The seven principles of creative problem solving*. Rocklin, CA: Prima Publishing, 1998.

Wall Street Journal. http://www.wsj.com

HIGH

This Factor measures various components of delivering results under first-time or tough situations. People high on this Factor pull things off under difficult conditions and build high-performing teams. They do so partially by personal drive and adaptability.

LOW

People low on this Factor have more trouble with first-time or difficult situations. They may have problems inspiring others or lack personal drive or presence. Perhaps as a consequence, results suffer when something new is needed.

SOME CAUSES

- ☐ Does the minimum to get by
- ☐ Doesn't like to lead or to be out front alone
- ☐ Flat personality
- ☐ Gets easily upset
- ☐ Lacks intensity and edge
- ☐ Last to try what's new
- ☐ Not ambitious
- ☐ Not comfortable with uncertainty and ambiguity
- ☐ Not resourceful
- ☐ Not well networked
- ☐ Too comfortable with what is

Factor IV

Factor IV

SKILLED

Can build a team through motivation and through the confidence the team has in him/her.

UNSKILLED

Has problems with team building; may lack take-charge skills, not be very motivating or fail to build confidence in others.

ITEMS

- ☐ 24. Can inspire a team to work hard.
- ☐ 51. Can state his/her case or viewpoint with energizing passion.
- ☐ 78. Can build and manage a high-performing team.

LEADERSHIP ARCHITECT® COMPETENCIES MOST ASSOCIATED WITH THIS DIMENSION

Strong

- ☐ 9. Command Skills
- ☐ 36. Motivating Others
- ☐ 39. Organizing
- ☐ 60. *Building Effective* Teams
- ☐ 65. *Managing* Vision and Purpose

Moderate

- ☐ 20. Directing Others
- ☐ 27. Informing
- ☐ 35. Managing and Measuring Work
- ☐ 56. Sizing Up People

24

Light

- ☐ 18. Delegation
- ☐ 21. *Managing* Diversity
- ☐ 29. Integrity and Trust
- ☐ 33. Listening
- ☐ 49. Presentation Skills

SOME CAUSES

- ☐ A loner
- ☐ Doesn't like to lead or be out front alone
- ☐ Doesn't listen
- ☐ Doesn't set standards or goals high enough
- ☐ Isn't motivated by winning
- ☐ Not a good role model for hard work
- ☐ Not achievement oriented
- ☐ Not approachable
- ☐ Not creative
- ☐ Not inspirational
- ☐ Not trustworthy
- ☐ Poor communicator
- ☐ Shy or withdrawn
- ☐ Too critical

24

THE MAP

Much more can be accomplished through others than by oneself. In our years of collecting data on managers and executives, individual skills are typically high, while team skills languish. Getting things done through others is key to success as a manager. Setting goals. Delegating. Measuring. Helping. Correcting. Urging. Rewarding. Celebrating. That's the cycle of inspiration.

SOME REMEDIES

☐ 1. Follow the rules of inspiring others. Communicate importance, celebrate wins, give people ways to measure themselves and see progress, set goals, provide autonomy, provide a variety of tasks. These are the proven winners to get people engaged in their work.

☐ 2. Play the motivation odds. The top motivators at work (unchanged during the past quarter century) are: job challenge, accomplishing something worthwhile, learning new things, personal development, and autonomy. Pay, friendliness, praise, and chance of promotion don't make the top 10.

☐ 3. Establish common cause. Nothing galvanizes people like a shared purpose, which is what holds any group together. Get everyone involved in sharing a common vision. Don't leave out the quiet or the reluctant. Repeatedly sell the logic of pulling together, listen, ask questions, invite suggestions to reach the outcome. Leave how things are to be done as open as possible. Specified sequences can be demotivating, even boring. People work harder under conditions of choice. Encourage experimentation.

☐ 4. Don't believe in teams? You're probably a strong individual achiever who doesn't like the mess and time expenditure of team processes. To change your thinking, observe and talk with three excellent team builders and ask them why they manage this way. Chances are they are not that different from you, as team building is not a common skill. Learn from others who probably had the same doubts that you do now.

24

☐ 5. Don't know how to build a team? Here are five characteristics of high-performance teams:

- They have a shared mind-set.

- They trust one another—cover for each other, pitch in, are candid, deal with issues directly.

- They have the talent collectively to do the job.

- They operate efficiently, doing the small things well—running meetings, assigning work, dealing with conflict.

- Most central to their excellence, they focus outside the team on customers and results. They do not focus much internally on atmosphere and happiness. This, however, is a characteristic of low-performing teams, who tend to delude themselves about their performance and focus on harmony.

☐ 6. Be a teacher. Always explain your thinking. Work out loud with them on a task. What do you see as important? How do you know? What questions are you asking? What steps are you following? Simply firing out solutions will make people more dependent at best.

☐ 7. Learn how to develop others. Developing direct reports and others is dead last in skill level among the 67 competencies of the LEADERSHIP ARCHITECT® and has been since we started collecting these data. To develop people, you have to follow the essential rules of development. They take a bit of time. Development is not simply sending someone to a course:

- Start with a portrait of the person's strengths and weaknesses. They can't grow if they are misinformed about themselves.

- Provide ongoing feedback from multiple sources.

- Give them progressively stretching tasks that are first-time and different for them. At least 70 percent of reported development occurs through challenging assignments that demand skill development. People don't grow from doing more of the same.

- Encourage them to think of themselves as learners, not just accomplishers. What are they learning that is new or different? What skills have grown in the last year? What have they learned that they can use in other situations?

- Use coursework, books, development partners, and mentoring to reinforce learning.

☐ 8. Work on your visual side. Learn storyboarding, a pictorial technique of representing a problem or process. Use mindmapping, a wonderfully branching way to plan, examine ideas, and simply think differently. Get some scenario training, then implement it with your team to come up with likely futures. Use flowcharting software packages. Close your eyes and see what the outcome would look like. Come up with an image or symbol that embodies the vision. People are much more likely to get excited by stories, symbols, and images than a white paper explaining the plan.

☐ 9. **(Workaround)** Delegate inspiration to your team. If you aren't going to do it, give them a chance. Be more participative than the natural you. Get them involved in everything the team does. Let them set goals and agree how to measure them. Let them do the measurement and determine the rewards. Let them celebrate. You can get out of being more inspirational yourself if you let others get totally involved.

☐ 10. **(Workaround)** Engage an internal or external coach to help you determine what to do. Use someone who is good at determining the best way to approach people and knows how to motivate and inspire others. In time some may rub off, but the important goal is to begin doing what needs to be done.

24

MORE HELP?

See *FYI For Your Improvement*™. We have coded each item to about 10 tips from the *FYI* book. To use this resource, the codes below refer to the chapter and then the tip number from the *FYI* book. For example, in item 24 below, 36-1,2,3 refers to Chapter 36—Motivating Others, tips 1,2 and 3. If you don't have a copy of *FYI*, it is available through Lominger at 952-345-3610 or www.lominger.com

24. Can inspire a team to work hard.
    36-1,2,3; 60-1,4,6; 110-1,2,4,9

51. Can state his/her case or viewpoint with energizing passion.
    1-6; 49-2,4; 57-9; 65-1,2,5,6; 67-4,7

78. Can build and manage a high-performing team.
    18-1; 19-1; 35-7; 36-1; 60-1,4,6; 110-1,2,4

JOBS THAT WOULD ADD SKILLS IN THIS DIMENSION

☐ Significant People Demands—requiring managing a large number of people, usually in dispersed structures.

☐ Start-ups—requiring forging a new team and initiating a variety of new and first-time initiatives on a tight timetable.

☐ Fix-its/Turnarounds—requiring making tough decisions impacting a variety of people and constituencies in a negative environment.

☐ Scale (large) Assignments—managing larger numbers of people, most of them remote and several layers deep.

☐ Scope (very broad) Assignments—requiring managing a variety of people from different functions and activities about a variety of topics.

☐ Influencing Without Authority—working across organizational boundaries without the positional power to command attention and compliance.

24

PART-TIME ASSIGNMENTS THAT WOULD ADD SKILLS IN THIS DIMENSION

☐ Manage a group of balky and resisting people through an unpopular change or project.

☐ Assemble a team of diverse people to accomplish a difficult task.

☐ Build a multifunctional or multidivisional project team to tackle a common business issue or problem.

☐ Manage a group of people involved in tackling a fix-it or turn-around project.

☐ Manage a group of "green," inexperienced people as their coach, teacher, guide, etc.

☐ Relaunch an existing product or service that's not doing well.

☐ Manage a group of people who are older and/or more experienced to accomplish a task.

☐ Manage a group of low-competence people through a task they couldn't do by themselves.

☐ Manage a group including former peers to accomplish a task.

☐ Be a change agent; create a symbol for change; lead the rallying cry; champion a significant change and implementation.

☐ Create employee involvement teams.

☐ Manage a group through a significant business crisis.

SUGGESTED READINGS

Belasco, James A. and Jerre Stead. *Soaring with the Phoenix—Renewing the vision, reviving the spirit, and re-creating the success of your company*. New York: Warner Books, 1999.

Bolton, Robert. *People skills: How to assert yourself, listen to others, and resolve conflicts*. New York: Simon & Schuster, 1986.

Caponigro, Jeffrey R. *The crisis counselor: The executive's guide to avoiding, managing, and thriving on crises that occur in all businesses*. Southfield, MI: Barker Business Books, Inc., 1998.

Daniels, Aubrey C. *Bringing out the best in people*. New York: McGraw-Hill, Inc., 1994.

24

Deeprose, Donna. *The team coach: Vital new skills for supervisors & managers in a team environment*. New York: American Management Association, 1995.

Fisher, Kimball, Steven Rayner, William Belgard and the Belgard-Fisher-Rayner Team. *Tips for teams: A ready reference for solving common team problems*. New York: McGraw-Hill, Inc., 1995.

Katzenbach, Jon R. and Douglas K. Smith. *The wisdom of teams: Creating the high-performance organization*. Boston: Harvard Business School Press, 1993.

Katzenbach, Jon R. and Douglas K. Smith. *The wisdom of teams: Creating the high-performance organization* [sound recording]. New York: Harper Audio, 1994.

Mitroff, I.I. and G. Anagnos. *Managing crises before they happen*. New York: AMACOM, 2001.

Mullen, James X. *The simple art of greatness: Building, managing and motivating a kick-ass workforce*. New York: Viking, 1995.

Robbins, Harvey and Michael Finley. *The new Why teams don't work: What goes wrong and how to make it right*. San Francisco: Berrett-Koehler Publishers, 2000.

Spitzer, Dean R. *Supermotivation*. New York: AMACOM, 1995.

24

DIMENSION 25
DELIVERS RESULTS

SKILLED

Performs well under first-time, changing or tough conditions.

UNSKILLED

Has problems with the new, unusual or the changing. Results may suffer.

ITEMS

- ☐ 25. Performs well under first-time conditions; isn't thrown by changing circumstances.
- ☐ 52. Has often pulled off things with limited resources
- ☐ 79. Performs well in tough situations; can be counted on.

LEADERSHIP ARCHITECT® COMPETENCIES MOST ASSOCIATED WITH THIS DIMENSION

Strong

- ☐ 9. Command Skills
- ☐ 39. Organizing
- ☐ 53. *Drive for* Results

Moderate

- ☐ 20. Directing Others
- ☐ 32. Learning on the Fly
- ☐ 51. Problem Solving
- ☐ 57. Standing Alone

25

Light

☐ 1. Action Oriented

☐ 16. *Timely* Decision Making

☐ 43. Perseverance

☐ 50. Priority Setting

☐ 52. Process Management

SOME CAUSES

☐ Avoids conflict

☐ Defensive

☐ Doesn't like to be first

☐ Gets upset easily

☐ Lazy

☐ Not ambitious

☐ Not resourceful

☐ Prefers past and proven solutions

☐ Slows down when things get tough

☐ Uncomfortable with uncertainty

THE MAP

After all is said and done, results are what count.

SOME REMEDIES

☐ 1. Use mental rehearsal for tough situations. Learn to recognize the clues that you're about to fall back on old behavior and be ready with a fresh strategy that you have decided in advance. If you know, for example, that a solution isn't working and you're likely to be questioned about it, be ready to engage others and get the benefit of their thinking.

☐ 2. Leading in first-time situations is risky. You have to defend what you're doing, so convince yourself first that you are on the right track. Be prepared to explain again and again. Lightning bolts from detractors, people unsettled by change, and people who will always say it could have been done differently, better, and cheaper. To prepare for this, think about the 10 objections that will come up and mentally rehearse how you will reply. Listen patiently to people's concerns, acknowledge them, then explain why you think the change will be beneficial. Attack positions, but not people.

☐ 3. Define the problem, don't put it in a familiar box so you can feel comfortable. What is it and what isn't it? How many causes can you think of? Are you stating things as facts that are really your opinion? Are you generalizing from an example or two? Use patterns and themes to define problems.

☐ 4. Don't expect to get it right the first time. If a situation is ambiguous, be incremental. Make some small decisions, get instant feedback, treat mistakes and failures as ways to learn. Focus on your third or fourth try, not the first.

☐ 5. First-time and tough situations call for resourcefulness. First-time means you haven't done exactly this before. So first, define what it is that needs to be done. Then set final and progress goals and measures. Next, try to lay out the work in incremental steps with the full expectation that this will change and evolve over time. Then find and bargain for the resources you will need to perform. Get the support you need and rally the team that will be working on the project. Delegate as much as possible. Celebrate incremental gains. Experiment and expect some false paths and mistakes. Have a process for instant correction of the plan. Make things up on the fly. Expect the unexpected. All the while, relentlessly drive toward the original goals.

☐ 6. Recognize your frustration and anxiety triggers. Initial anxious responses last 45 to 60 seconds. They are marked by your characteristic emotional response. Learn to recognize your unique triggers: Voice go up? Shift in your chair? Harsh thoughts? Once

25

181

you have figured out your triggers, ask why. Is it ego? Extra work? People you dislike or think are lazy? For each grouping, figure out what would be a more mature response. If it's too late, count to 10 or ask a clarifying question. Stall until the initial burst of glucose subsides.

☐ 7. It's all in a day's work: going from a tense meeting to a celebration for a notable accomplishment. Think of your day as a series of transitions. For a week, monitor your gear-shifting behavior at work and at home. What transitions give you the most trouble? The least? Why? Practice gear-shifting transitions. On the way between activities, think about the transition you're making and the frame of mind required to make it.

☐ 8. Give up too soon on an idea? If you have trouble going back the second or third time, then switch approaches. For example, you could meet with all stakeholders, a single key stakeholder, present the idea to a group, call in an expert to buttress your innovation, or project various scenarios showing the value of the idea.

☐ 9. Have trouble getting it done across boundaries? Don't just ask for things; find some common ground where you can provide help. What do the peers you need need? If it affects them negatively, you can appeal to the common good, trade something, or figure out some way to minimize the impact. Go into these relationships with a trading mentality, not a handout mentality.

☐ 10. **(Workaround)** Stay out of first-time situations. If you are content to be you and not perform well in new and different situations, keep yourself out of them. Play with the cards you have. Turn down jobs and assignments that involve fresh challenges. Concentrate on being a very strong performer in the areas you are comfortable in. Work on your functional expertise. Specialize doing a little better tomorrow what you do well today. Leave cutting a path through the jungle to others more bold and adventurous.

25

MORE HELP?

See *FYI For Your Improvement™*. We have coded each item to about 10 tips from the *FYI* book. To use this resource, the codes below refer to the chapter and then the tip number from the *FYI* book. For example, in item 25 below, 2-1,2,4,5,7 refers to Chapter 2—*Dealing with* Ambiguity, tips 1,2,4,5 and 7. If you don't have a copy of *FYI*, it is available through Lominger at 952-345-3610 or www.lominger.com

25. Performs well under first-time conditions; isn't thrown by changing circumstances.
2-1,2,4,5,7; 32-1,4,9; 40-1; 51-5

52. Has often pulled off things with limited resources.
53-1,2,3,4,5,6,7,8,9,10

79. Performs well in tough situations; can be counted on.
9-1,2,3,4,5,10; 12-7; 13-2; 40-9; 53-1

JOBS THAT WOULD ADD SKILLS IN THIS DIMENSION

☐ Fix-its/Turnarounds—requiring making things happen on a tight schedule that are new and different in a negative environment.

☐ Start-ups—requiring forging a new team and acting on several simultaneous fronts with few precedents to go on.

☐ Chair of Projects/Task Forces—requiring finding new and effective solutions under tight deadlines and high visibility on an issue that matters to people higher up.

☐ Scope (very broad) Assignments—requiring getting things done across diverse units.

☐ Influencing Without Authority—getting things done across organizational boundaries without the power to command attention and compliance.

☐ Scale (large) Assignments—managing larger numbers of people and being responsible for significant outcomes.

25

PART-TIME ASSIGNMENTS THAT WOULD ADD SKILLS IN THIS DIMENSION

☐ Manage a group of people involved in tackling a fix-it or turnaround project.

☐ Relaunch an existing product or service that's not doing well.

☐ Manage a group of balky and resisting people through an unpopular change or project.

☐ Help shut down a plant, regional office, product line, business, operation, etc.

☐ Manage a group through a significant business crisis.

☐ Assemble a team of diverse people to accomplish a difficult task.

☐ Launch a new product, service, or process.

☐ Manage a group of people in a rapidly expanding operation.

☐ Build a multifunctional project team to tackle a common business issue or problem.

☐ Take on a tough and undoable project, one where others who have tried it have failed.

☐ Manage a group of low-competence people through a task they couldn't do by themselves.

☐ Manage the renovation of an office, floor, building, meeting room, warehouse, etc.

☐ Plan for and start up something small (secretarial pool, athletic program, suggestion system, program, etc.).

☐ Integrate diverse systems, processes, or procedures across decentralized and/or dispersed units.

☐ Manage a deep cost-cutting project.

25

SUGGESTED READINGS

Bolton, Robert. *People skills: How to assert yourself, listen to others and resolve conflicts*. New York: Simon & Schuster, 1986.

Bernstein, Albert J. and Sydney Craft Rozen. *Sacred bull: The inner obstacles that hold you back at work and how to overcome them*. New York: Wiley, 1994.

Bossidy, Larry, Ram Charan and Charles Burck (Contributor). *Execution: The discipline of getting things done*. New York: Crown Business Publishing, 2002.

Caponigro, Jeffrey R. *The crisis counselor: The executive's guide to avoiding, managing, and thriving on crises that occur in all businesses*. Southfield, MI: Barker Business Books, Inc., 1998.

Cox, Danny and John Hoover. *Leadership when the heat's on*. New York: McGraw-Hill, Inc., 1992.

Dimitrius, Jo-Ellan and Mark Mazzarella. *Reading people: How to understand people and predict their behavior— Anytime, anyplace*. New York: Random House, 1998.

DuBrin, Andrew J. *Your own worst enemy*. New York: AMACOM, 1992.

Kheel, Theodore W. *The keys to conflict resolution—Proven methods of resolving disputes voluntarily*. New York: Four Walls Eight Windows, 1999.

Kotter, John P. and Dan S. Cohen. *The heart of change: Real-life stories of how people change their organizations*. Watertown, MA: Harvard Business School Press, 2002.

Lee, John H. with Bill Stott. *Facing the fire: Experiencing and expressing anger appropriately*. New York: Bantam Books, 1993.

Loehr, James E. *Stress for success*. New York: Times Business, 1997.

Meyers, Gerald C. with John Holusha. *When it hits the fan: Managing the nine crises of business*. Boston: Houghton Mifflin, 1986.

Neuhauser, Peg. *Tribal warfare in organizations*. New York: Harper & Row, 1988.

Van Slyke, Erik J. *Listening to conflict*. New York: AMACOM, 1999.

25

25

DIMENSION 26
DRIVE

SKILLED

Works hard on many fronts; high standards of excellence.

UNSKILLED

May have difficulty with many balls in the air at once; may not be willing to make personal sacrifices, or may have lower standards of excellence than needed.

ITEMS

☐ 26. Can work on many things at once; is a multi-track person.

☐ 53. Is willing to work hard and make personal sacrifices to get ahead.

☐ 80. Has high internal standards of excellence in addition to being tuned to outside standards.

LEADERSHIP ARCHITECT® COMPETENCIES MOST ASSOCIATED WITH THIS DIMENSION

Strong

☐ 1. Action Oriented

☐ 43. Perseverance

☐ 53. *Drive for* Results

Moderate

☐ 6. Career Ambition

☐ 32. Learning on the Fly

☐ 50. Priority Setting

☐ 57. Standing Alone

26

Light

- ☐ 2. *Dealing with* Ambiguity
- ☐ 16. *Timely* Decision Making
- ☐ 35. Managing and Measuring Work

SOME CAUSES

- ☐ Does the minimum to get by
- ☐ Has low standards
- ☐ Isn't inspired by winning
- ☐ Isn't motivated by what is done at work
- ☐ Lazy
- ☐ Lives in a comfort zone
- ☐ Not ambitious
- ☐ Puts a high value on balance between work and personal life
- ☐ Self-centered and selfish
- ☐ Single-tracked
- ☐ Tires easily

THE MAP

Drive and inspiration make the world go around. Finding the passion to perform is one key to success and accomplishment. Anyone will work harder when they are working on something they are passionate about. Besides personal passion, it is the role of the manager and leader to help others find their passion. And in some cases, to create passion where none existed before. Passion eases the difficulty of working on several things at once. It adds persistence.

26

SOME REMEDIES

☐ 1. Lost your passion for the job? Make a list of what you like to do and don't like to do. Concentrate on doing a few things you like each day. See if you can delegate or trade for more desirable activities. Do your least preferred activities first. Focus not on the activity but your sense of accomplishment. Volunteer for task forces and projects that would be more interesting for you.

☐ 2. Get out of your comfort zone. Find an activity that goes against your natural likes and try it. Up your risk comfort. Start small so you can recover quickly. Pick a few smaller tasks or challenges and build the skill bit by bit. For example, if strategy is your area, write a strategic plan for your unit and show it to people to get feedback, then write a second draft. Devise a strategy for turning one of your hobbies (i.e., photography) into a business.

☐ 3. Unwilling to make sacrifices? Many people turn down career opportunities based upon current life comforts only to regret it later when they are passed by. Perhaps you love what you do now and can't imagine doing anything else. The problem with that is needs change, and if you don't, your prospects are not bright. That scary and unappealing new job will add new skills and variety to your resume at the least. Most successful people have taken any number of jobs which didn't appeal but which did broaden them.

☐ 4. Perhaps you don't know how successful careers are really built. What has staying power is performing in a variety of jobs, not more of the same jobs, having a few notable strengths, and seeking new tasks that you don't know how to do. A successful career is built on stress and newness. Talk to some successful people in your organization and hear how random their careers likely have been. Read *The Lessons of Experience, High Flyers,* and *Breaking the Glass Ceiling* to see how successful executives grew over time.

26

☐ 5. Take more risks. Research indicates that more successful people have made more mistakes than the less successful. You can't learn anything if you're not trying anything new. Start small, experiment a bit. Go for small wins so you can recover quickly if you miss and, more important, learn from the results. Start with the easiest challenge, then work up to the tougher ones.

☐ 6. Revisit your priorities. Some people get results but don't focus on the most important priorities. Successful managers typically spend half their time on two or three key priorities. They don't flit from task to task, working on whatever comes up. They give attention, but not too much, to lesser priorities. The key questions are: What should you be spending half your time on? Can you name five priorities that are less critical than these? If you can't, then you are not differentiating well.

☐ 7. Don't try to get it right the first time. If a situation is ambiguous, be incremental. Make some small decisions, get instant feedback, treat mistakes and failures as ways to learn. Focus on your third or fourth try, not the first.

☐ 8. Why aren't you delegating? Are you a perfectionist, wanting everything to be just so? Unrealistic expectations? Won't risk giving out tough work? If this is you, expect career trouble. Better managers delegate more and work shorter hours than managers who try to control most things. The keys are setting priorities, providing help, and designing work flows, not your personal effort. Communicate, set time frames and goals, and get out of the way. Be very clear on what and when, be very open on how. People are more motivated when they can determine the how themselves. Encourage them to try things. Delegate complete tasks, not pieces. Allow more time than it would take you to do it.

☐ 9. Use goals for yourself and others to build passion and drive. Almost everyone is motivated by achieving goals. Especially if they have had a hand in setting them. Make goals small and reasonably achievable. Set incremental goals or process goals.

Don't just set the outcome or end goals. Create a goal process so there can be a lot of celebrating along the way.

☐ 10. **(Workaround)** If you don't want to work harder, work smarter. Learn the technologies of work process design. Study things like TQM, process engineering, ISO, and Six Sigma. Use tools that make designing and managing work easier. Get it right the first time so you don't have to do rework. Hire the best people and delegate. Look for the easier assignments that still fit into your career path. Work for good companies and good bosses so there is less noise and distraction. Compromise on pay and promotions. If you chose to lay back and not push performance to the higher levels, your rewards will be less and your promotions less frequent.

MORE HELP?

See *FYI For Your Improvement*™. We have coded each item to about 10 tips from the *FYI* book. To use this resource, the codes below refer to the chapter and then the tip number from the *FYI* book. For example, in item 26 below, 2-1,2,3,4,10 refers to Chapter 2—*Dealing with* Ambiguity, tips 1,2,3,4 and 10. If you don't have a copy of *FYI*, it is available through Lominger at 952-345-3610 or www.lominger.com

26. Can work on many things at once; is a multi-track person.
2-1,2,3,4,10; 18-1; 40-1,9; 50-2,3

53. Is willing to work hard and make personal sacrifices to get ahead.
1-6,10; 6-1,3,8; 9-1,9,10; 118-7,8

80. Has high internal standards of excellence in addition to being tuned to outside standards.
1-6,10; 6-3,5,8; 57-8; 101-2,3,6; 118-1

26

JOBS THAT WOULD ADD SKILLS IN THIS DIMENSION

☐ Fix-its/Turnarounds—requiring making tough decision impacting a variety of people and constituencies in a tough environment under negative conditions.

☐ Start-ups—requiring forging a new team and initiating a number of simultaneous actions with little guidance from the past under a tight time frame.

☐ Staff to Line Shift—involving moving from a staff role to a line job where there is a more easily determined bottom line or direct measurement of results.

☐ Chair of Projects/Task Forces—requiring finding new and effective solutions under tight deadlines and high visibility on an issue that matters to people higher up.

☐ Influencing Without Authority—communicating across organizational boundaries without the positional power to command attention and compliance.

☐ Out of Home Country Assignments—requiring getting things done on your own with less direct support from headquarters.

PART-TIME ASSIGNMENTS THAT WOULD ADD SKILLS IN THIS DIMENSION

☐ Manage a group of people involved in tackling a fix-it or turnaround project.

☐ Manage a group of balky and resisting people through an unpopular change or project.

☐ Relaunch an existing product or service that's not doing well.

☐ Take on a tough and undoable project, one where others who have tried it have failed.

☐ Plan a new site for a building (plant, field office, headquarters, etc.).

☐ Manage the renovation of an office, floor, building, meeting room, warehouse, etc.

26

☐ Launch a new product, service, or process.

☐ Manage a group of people in a rapidly expanding operation.

☐ Assemble a team of diverse people to accomplish a difficult task.

☐ Manage a group through a significant business crisis.

☐ Plan for and start up something small (secretarial pool, athletic program, suggestion system, program, etc.).

☐ Build a multifunctional project team to tackle a common business issue or problem.

☐ Take on a task you dislike or hate to do.

☐ Plan a major new off-site meeting, conference, convention, trade show, event, etc.

☐ Manage a dissatisfied internal or external customer; troubleshoot a performance or quality problem with a product or service.

SUGGESTED READINGS

Bernstein, Albert J. and Sydney Craft Rozen. *Sacred bull: The inner obstacles that hold you back at work and how to overcome them*. New York: Wiley, 1994.

Bolles, Richard N. *What color is your parachute?* Berkeley, CA: Ten Speed Press, 2004.

Bossidy, Larry, Ram Charan and Charles Burck (Contributor). *Execution: The discipline of getting things done*. New York: Crown Business Publishing, 2002.

Champy, James and Nitin Nohria. *The arc of ambition*. Cambridge, MA: Perseus Publishing, 2001.

DuBrin, Andrew J. *Your own worst enemy*. New York: AMACOM, 1992.

26

Lombardo, Michael and Robert Eichinger. *The leadership machine*. Minneapolis: Lominger, 2002.

McCall, M.W. *High Flyers: Developing the next generation of leaders*. Boston: Harvard Business School Press, 1998.

McCall, M.W., M. Lombardo and A. Morrison. *The lessons of experience*. Lexington, MA: Lexington Books, 1988.

Morrison, A., R. White and E. VanVelsor. *Breaking the glass ceiling: Can women reach the top of America's largest corporations?* Reading, MA: Addison-Wesley Publishing Company, 1987, rev. 1992.

Searing, Jill A. and Anne B. Lovett. *The career prescription: How to stop sabotaging your career and put it on a winning track*. Englewood Cliffs, NJ: Prentice Hall, 1995.

26

DIMENSION 27
PRESENCE

SKILLED

You know he/she is around; self-assured, can be passionate about beliefs.

UNSKILLED

May not show or lacks self-confidence; may be reluctant to step forth, or be seen as low key.

ITEMS

- ☐ 27. People feel more confident when this person is in charge.
- ☐ 54. Exudes self-confidence.
- ☐ 81. Has a significant, noticeable presence.

LEADERSHIP ARCHITECT® COMPETENCIES MOST ASSOCIATED WITH THIS DIMENSION

Strong

- ☐ 9. Command Skills
- ☐ 49. Presentation Skills
- ☐ 57. Standing Alone

Moderate

- ☐ 20. Directing Others
- ☐ 31. Interpersonal Savvy
- ☐ 36. Motivating Others
- ☐ 39. Organizing
- ☐ 65. *Managing* Vision and Purpose

27

Light

- ☐ 11. Composure
- ☐ 12. Conflict Management
- ☐ 16. *Timely* Decision Making
- ☐ 34. Managerial Courage
- ☐ 53. *Drive for* Results

SOME CAUSES

- ☐ A loner
- ☐ Cold and impassionate
- ☐ Flat style
- ☐ Lacks edge
- ☐ No leadership experience or background
- ☐ Not engaging
- ☐ Not self-confident
- ☐ Poor communicator
- ☐ Stays in the background
- ☐ Withdrawn and quiet

THE MAP

If you want to lead, you have to act the part. Lack of confidence, inability to handle push back, and hanging back don't project the presence necessary to lead change. People need to know you are around and what you stand for. Presence creates receptivity in others. They will stop and listen.

27

SOME REMEDIES

☐ 1. Build up your confidence. Take a course or work with a tutor to build your confidence in one area at a time. Focus on the strengths you do have; think of ways you can use them to your benefit. If you're an expert in an area, imagine yourself calmly delivering key maps.

☐ 2. Leading is greatly aided by presence. You have to look and sound like a leader. Study people who have a commanding presence. Pay attention to their voice modulation, change of pace, eye contact, gestures, and so on. Do you dress the part? Do you sound confident? Do you complain or do you project an image of someone who solves problems? Giving presentations and looking the part is a known technology. Go to a course; join Toastmasters. Get coaching from an acting director. Act a scene in a pretend play called "Presence."

☐ 3. When speaking to someone or a group, state your message or purpose in a single sentence, then outline your pitch around three to five things that support this thesis and that you want people to remember. Consider what someone should be able to say 15 minutes after you finish. Don't try to tell the audience all you know, even if they are well-informed on the topic. You are giving a persuasive argument or communicating key information; it's not a lecture. Drowning people in detail will lose even the knowledgeable and the interested. Practice out loud. Writing out a pitch or argument isn't useful until you say it. Writing sounds stilted when spoken because the cadence of speech and sentence length is generally quite different.

☐ 4. Leading is risky. You have to defend what you're doing, so convince yourself first that you are on the right track. Be prepared to explain again and again. Lightning bolts from detractors, people unsettled by change, and people who will always say it could have been done differently, better, and cheaper. To prepare for this, think about the 10 objections that will come up, and mentally rehearse how you will reply. Listen patiently to people's

27

197

concerns, acknowledge them, then explain why you think the change will be beneficial. Attack positions, but not people.

☐ 5. Be more real. Seek critical feedback. Others view people who seek critical feedback more positively. People who seek only positive feedback get the opposite response. The former shows willingness to improve. The latter is often seen as defensiveness and a disinterest in really knowing oneself. Disclose more. If you deny, minimize, or excuse away mistakes and shortcomings, take a chance and admit that you're imperfect like everyone else. Let your inside thoughts out in the open more often. Take personal responsibility. Admit mistakes matter of factly, inform everyone potentially affected, learn from it so the mistake isn't repeated, then move on. Successful people make lots of mistakes. All of this adds to a positive presence.

☐ 6. Listen more. Do you really know how others see the issue or do you just tell and sell? Do you even know if it is important to them? Don't interrupt. Don't suggest words or solutions when they pause. Don't cut them off by saying, "I already know that," "I've heard that before," or the dreaded "But I know that won't work." Be a two-way person. Practice reciprocity. Try to follow the rule of exchange. They get something, you get something. Build your presence by being more open, sharing, and giving.

☐ 7. Eliminate poor speech habits, such as using the same words repeatedly, using filler words like "uh" and "you know," speaking too rapidly or forcefully, or going into so much detail that people can't follow the map. Avoid condescending terms like "What you need to understand" or "This is the third time...." Both imply the receiver is either stupid or unwilling. Don't use words that are personal, blaming, or autocratic. Outline arguments. Know the three things you're trying to say and say them succinctly. Others can always ask questions if something is unclear.

☐ 8. Using acting as a model for building presence, there are several aspects of the stage performance that enter into the actor's skills:

- The first is the significance of the entrance. People tend to form short-term impressions based on little other than the manner of entrance, the physical characteristics of the actor, and the words and non-verbal behaviors in the first few moments. Think about the impression you want to leave. Vision your entrance. Does it leave the message you intend. Do you look, act, and sound your intended presence?

- Next is establishing your voice. Voice has three elements. The first is the actual delivery voice. Volume. Tone. Speed. Language. Articulation. The second is non-verbals. Do your non-verbals (gestures, posture, facial expressions, movement) align with your message? The next is content. Are you confident and knowledgeable? Is it apparent that you know what you are talking about? Do you know your lines?

- The next element of presence is audience engagement. How do you intend to engage the audience? Is this going to be participative? Does the audience have a role? Do they know what it is you expect? Are you in command of your audience?

- The last element of presence is the exit. How do you intend to wrap things up? Do you have a strong close? Have you planned how you are going to end and finish by leaving your audience with the thoughts and conclusions you intended?

For the actor, these are the elements of creating a strong stage presence. It's not that different in the world of work. Everything matters. Taken all together, they build presence.

27

☐ 9. Lack boldness? Tired of what you do? Find something that needs changing for which you have some enthusiasm. Appoint yourself as champion of the change. Throw out trial balloons to see if your notion spurs some interest. Find an experimenter to go in with you. Bring in a heavy expert. Plant seeds at every opportunity.

☐ 10. **(Workaround)** If you are not blessed with presence and do not want to work to increase it, learn to market other aspects of yourself. Set up a marketing plan. What are you good at? What have you accomplished? What would others be interested to know about you? How can you help them be more successful? In order to make up for a lack of presence, you need substance and content. Through those aspects of yourself, you can get respect and probably get a following of people interested in working with and for you.

MORE HELP?

See *FYI For Your Improvement*™. We have coded each item to about 10 tips from the *FYI* book. To use this resource, the codes below refer to the chapter and then the tip number from the *FYI* book. For example, in item 27 below, 1-1,4 refers to Chapter 1—Action Oriented, tips 1 and 4. If you don't have a copy of *FYI*, it is available through Lominger at 952-345-3610 or www.lominger.com

27. People feel more confident when this person is in charge.
1-1,4; 9-1,3,4,5,8,10; 53-1; 60-1

54. Exudes self-confidence.
1-4; 9-1,2,3,4,5,8,10; 107-1; 108-2

81. Has a significant, noticeable presence.
1-4; 8-1; 9-1,2,3,5,10; 34-7; 107-1; 108-2

27

JOBS THAT WOULD ADD SKILLS IN THIS DIMENSION

☐ Crisis or Change Manager—requiring quick, tough-minded decisions under tight time pressure with a low level of consultation and more resting on one person's thinking and actions than is typical.

☐ Fix-its/Turnarounds—requiring making tough decisions impacting a variety of people and constituencies on a tight schedule with little room for error and the weight of the thinking and plan resting on one person.

☐ Start-ups—requiring forging a new team and initiating a number of simultaneous actions with little guidance from the past under a tight time frame with the major burden of thinking and actions on one person.

☐ Scale (large) Assignments—impacting larger numbers of people with many of them remote and dispersed.

☐ Chair of Projects/Task Forces—requiring finding new and effective solutions under tight deadlines and high visibility on an issue that matters to people higher up.

☐ Significant People Demands—requiring managing a large number of people usually in dispersed structures.

PART-TIME ASSIGNMENTS THAT WOULD ADD SKILLS IN THIS DIMENSION

☐ Manage a group of people involved in tackling a fix-it or turnaround project.

☐ Relaunch an existing product or service that's not doing well.

☐ Manage a group of balky and resisting people through an unpopular change or project.

☐ Manage a group through a significant business crisis.

☐ Take on a tough and undoable project, one where others who have tried it have failed.

27

☐ Assemble a team of diverse people to accomplish a difficult task, or build a multifunctional project team to tackle a common business issue or problem.

☐ Manage a group including former peers to accomplish a task.

☐ Integrate diverse systems, processes, or procedures across decentralized and/or dispersed units.

☐ Manage a group of people who are older and/or more experienced to accomplish a task.

☐ Prepare and present a proposal of some consequence to top management.

☐ Be a change agent; create a symbol for change; lead the rallying cry; champion a significant change and implementation.

☐ Manage a group of "green," inexperienced people as their coach, teacher, guide, etc.

☐ Manage an ad hoc, temporary group of low-competence people through a task they couldn't do by themselves.

☐ Handle a tough negotiation with an internal or external client or customer.

SUGGESTED READINGS

Bolton, Robert and Dorothy Grover Bolton. *People styles at work.* New York: AMACOM, 1996.

Collins, Patrick J. *Say it with confidence.* New York: Prentice Hall, 1998.

Cox, Danny and John Hoover. *Leadership when the heat's on.* New York: McGraw-Hill, Inc., 1992.

Dimitrius, Jo-Ellan and Mark Mazzarella. *Reading people: How to understand people and predict their behavior—Anytime, anyplace.* New York: Random House, 1998.

Dowis, R. *The lost art of the great speech.* New York: AMACOM, 2000.

27

DuBrin, Andrew J. *Your own worst enemy.* New York: AMACOM, 1992.

Griffin, Jack. *How to say it at work: Putting yourself across with power words, phrases, body language and communication secrets.* Paramus, NJ: Prentice Hall, 1998.

Hendricks, William, Micki Holliday, Recie Mobley and Kristy Steinbrecher. *Secrets of power presentations.* Franklin Lakes, NJ: Career Press, 1996.

Kheel, Theodore W. *The keys to conflict resolution—Proven methods of resolving disputes voluntarily.* New York: Four Walls Eight Windows, 1999.

Kiser, A. Glenn. *Masterful facilitation: Becoming a catalyst for meaningful change.* New York: AMACOM, 1998.

Lee, John H. with Bill Stott. *Facing the fire: Experiencing and expressing anger appropriately.* New York: Bantam Books, 1993.

Presentations Magazine. www.presentations.com

Rafe, Stephen C. *How to be prepared to think on your feet.* New York: HarperBusiness, 1990.

27

27

MY PERSONAL DEVELOPMENT PLAN

SECTION 1:   MY BEFORE AND AFTER PICTURE

SECTION 2:   SOME CAUSES FOR ME

SECTION 3:   LEARNINGS FROM "THE MAP" FOR ME

SECTION 4:   MY DEVELOPMENT REMEDIES AND
ACTION PLANS

SECTION 5:   JOBS THAT WOULD HELP ME ADD SKILLS

SECTION 6:   PART-TIME ASSIGNMENTS THAT WOULD
HELP ME ADD SKILLS

SECTION 7:   MY SUGGESTED READINGS

SECTION 1 – MY BEFORE AND AFTER PICTURE

Look to the Unskilled Definitions (from–I am more like this now) and the Skilled Definitions (to–I would like to be more like this in the future).

Dimension #: _____

1. From: _____

_____

_____

To: _____

_____

Dimension #: _____

2. From: _____

_____

_____

To: _____

_____

_____

Dimension #: _____

3. From: _____

_____

_____

To: _____

_____

Dimension #: _____

4. From: _____

_____

_____

To: _____

_____

Dimension #: _____

5. From: _____

_____

_____

To: _____

_____

SECTION 1 – MY BEFORE AND AFTER PICTURE
Look to the Unskilled Definitions (from–I am more like this now) and the Skilled Definitions (to–I would like to be more like this in the future).

Dimension #: _____

1. From: _____
   _____
   _____

   To: _____
   _____

Dimension #: _____

2. From: _____
   _____
   _____

   To: _____
   _____
   _____

Dimension #: _____

3. From: _____
   _____
   _____

   To: _____
   _____

Dimension #: _____

4. From: _____
   _____
   _____

   To: _____
   _____

Dimension #: _____

5. From: _____
   _____
   _____

   To: _____
   _____

SECTION 2 – SOME CAUSES FOR ME
(Why am I like this? Why do I do things this way?) Look to "Some Causes" for clues.

Dimension #:____ 1. _____

Comments: _____

_____

_____

_____

Dimension #:____ 2. _____

Comments: _____

_____

_____

_____

Dimension #:____ 3. _____

Comments: _____

_____

_____

_____

Dimension #:____ 4. _____

Comments: _____

_____

_____

_____

Dimension #:____ 5. _____

Comments: _____

_____

_____

_____

SECTION 2 – SOME CAUSES FOR ME
(Why am I like this? Why do I do things this way?) Look to "Some Causes" for clues.

Dimension #:___ 1._____

Comments: _____

_____

_____

_____

Dimension #:___ 2._____

Comments: _____

_____

_____

_____

Dimension #:___ 3._____

Comments: _____

_____

_____

_____

Dimension #:___ 4._____

Comments: _____

_____

_____

_____

Dimension #:___ 5._____

Comments: _____

_____

_____

_____

SECTION 3 – LEARNINGS FROM "THE MAP" FOR ME

Dimension #: _____

1. _____

Dimension #: _____

2. _____

Dimension #: _____

3. _____

Dimension #: _____

4. _____

Dimension #: _____

5. _____

SECTION 3 – LEARNINGS FROM "THE MAP" FOR ME

Dimension #: _____

1. _____

Dimension #: _____

2. _____

Dimension #: _____

3. _____

Dimension #: _____

4. _____

Dimension #: _____

5. _____

SECTION 4 – MY DEVELOPMENT REMEDIES AND ACTION PLANS

Dimension #: _____

Tip # _____ _____

_____

_____

_____

Plan: _____

_____

_____

_____

Dimension #: _____

Tip # _____ _____

_____

_____

_____

Plan: _____

_____

_____

_____

Dimension #: _____

Tip # _____ _____

_____

_____

_____

Plan: _____

_____

_____

_____

Dimension #: _____

Tip # _____ _____

_____

_____

_____

Plan: _____

_____

_____

_____

SECTION 4 – MY DEVELOPMENT REMEDIES AND ACTION PLANS *continued*

Dimension #: _____

Tip # _____ _____
_____
_____
_____

Plan: _____
_____
_____
_____

Dimension #: _____

Tip # _____ _____
_____
_____
_____

Plan: _____
_____
_____
_____

Dimension #: _____

Tip # _____ _____
_____
_____
_____

Plan:_____
_____
_____
_____

Dimension #: _____

Tip # _____ _____
_____
_____
_____

Plan: _____
_____
_____
_____

SECTION 4 – MY DEVELOPMENT REMEDIES AND ACTION PLANS

Dimension #: _____

Tip # _____ _____

_____

_____

_____

Plan: _____

_____

_____

_____

Dimension #: _____

Tip # _____ _____

_____

_____

_____

Plan: _____

_____

_____

_____

Dimension #: _____

Tip # _____ _____

_____

_____

_____

Plan: _____

_____

_____

_____

Dimension #: _____

Tip # _____ _____

_____

_____

_____

Plan: _____

_____

_____

_____

SECTION 4 – MY DEVELOPMENT REMEDIES AND ACTION PLANS *continued*

Dimension #: _____

Tip # _____ _____

_____

_____

_____

Plan: _____

_____

_____

_____

Dimension #: _____

Tip # _____ _____

_____

_____

_____

Plan: _____

_____

_____

_____

Dimension #: _____

Tip # _____ _____

_____

_____

_____

Plan: _____

_____

_____

_____

Dimension #: _____

Tip # _____ _____

_____

_____

_____

Plan: _____

_____

_____

_____

SECTION 5 – LEARNING FROM FULL-TIME JOBS THAT WILL HELP ME DEVELOP MY SKILLS

Write in Dimension Numbers Below

		Total Times ✔'d	*My Rank Order of Best Jobs for Me*
Chair of Projects/ Task Forces	☐☐☐☐☐☐☐	___	☐
Crisis or Change Manager	☐☐☐☐☐☐☐	___	☐
Cross Moves	☐☐☐☐☐☐☐	___	☐
Fix-its/ Turnarounds	☐☐☐☐☐☐☐	___	☐
Heavy Strategic Demands	☐☐☐☐☐☐☐	___	☐
Influencing Without Authority	☐☐☐☐☐☐☐	___	☐
Line to Staff Switches	☐☐☐☐☐☐☐	___	☐
Out of Home Country Assignments	☐☐☐☐☐☐☐	___	☐
Scale (large) Assignments	☐☐☐☐☐☐☐	___	☐
Scope (very broad) Assignments	☐☐☐☐☐☐☐	___	☐
Significant People Demands	☐☐☐☐☐☐☐	___	☐
Staff to Line Shift	☐☐☐☐☐☐☐	___	☐
Start-ups	☐☐☐☐☐☐☐	___	☐

217

SECTION 5 – LEARNING FROM FULL-TIME JOBS THAT WILL HELP ME DEVELOP MY SKILLS

Write in Dimension Numbers Below

	__ __ __ __ __ __ __	Total Times ✔'d	*My Rank Order of Best Jobs for Me*
Chair of Projects/ Task Forces	☐☐☐☐☐☐☐	___	☐
Crisis or Change Manager	☐☐☐☐☐☐☐	___	☐
Cross Moves	☐☐☐☐☐☐☐	___	☐
Fix-its/ Turnarounds	☐☐☐☐☐☐☐	___	☐
Heavy Strategic Demands	☐☐☐☐☐☐☐	___	☐
Influencing Without Authority	☐☐☐☐☐☐☐	___	☐
Line to Staff Switches	☐☐☐☐☐☐☐	___	☐
Out of Home Country Assignments	☐☐☐☐☐☐☐	___	☐
Scale (large) Assignments	☐☐☐☐☐☐☐	___	☐
Scope (very broad) Assignments	☐☐☐☐☐☐☐	___	☐
Significant People Demands	☐☐☐☐☐☐☐	___	☐
Staff to Line Shift	☐☐☐☐☐☐☐	___	☐
Start-ups	☐☐☐☐☐☐☐	___	☐

SECTION 6 – LEARNING FROM PART-TIME ASSIGNMENTS
Which Assignment would be useful and practical for me?

_____ Assignment   _____
                       _____
                       _____
                       _____

_____ Assignment   _____
                       _____
                       _____
                       _____

_____ Assignment   _____
                       _____
                       _____
                       _____

_____ Assignment   _____
                       _____
                       _____
                       _____

_____ Assignment   _____
                       _____
                       _____
                       _____

SECTION 6 – LEARNING FROM PART-TIME ASSIGNMENTS
Which Assignment would be useful and practical for me?

_____ Assignment

_____
_____
_____
_____

_____ Assignment

_____
_____
_____
_____

_____ Assignment

_____
_____
_____
_____

_____ Assignment

_____
_____
_____
_____

_____ Assignment

_____
_____
_____
_____

SECTION 7 – MY SUGGESTED READINGS

Dimension #: _____

Readings: _____

_____

_____

_____

Dimension #: _____

Readings: _____

_____

_____

_____

_____

Dimension #: _____

Readings: _____

_____

_____

_____

Dimension #:_____

Readings: _____

_____

_____

_____

Dimension #: _____

Readings: _____

_____

_____

_____

SECTION 7 – MY SUGGESTED READINGS

Dimension #: _____

Readings: _____

_____

_____

_____

Dimension #: _____

Readings: _____

_____

_____

_____

_____

Dimension #: _____

Readings: _____

_____

_____

_____

Dimension #: _____

Readings: _____

_____

_____

_____

Dimension #: _____

Readings: _____

_____

_____

_____

APPENDIX B

COMPETENCY SUMMARY

TOP 22 LEADERSHIP ARCHITECT® COMPETENCIES MOST ASSOCIATED WITH CHOICES ARCHITECT® 2ND EDITION ITEMS

1. *Dealing with* Ambiguity (2)
2. Problem Solving (51)
3. Learning on the Fly (32)
4. Perspective (46)
5. Conflict Management (12)
6. Sizing Up People (56)
7. Listening (33)
8. *Dealing with* Paradox (40)
9. Standing Alone (57)
10. Personal Learning (45)
11. Patience (41)
12. Process Management (52)
13. Creativity (14)
14. Understanding Others (64)
15. Composure (11)
16. Motivating Others (36)
17. Organizing (39)
18. Self-Knowledge (55)
19. Command Skills (9)
20. Priority Setting (50)
21. *Managing* Diversity (21)
22. *Timely* Decision Making (16)

Want to learn more about the LEADERSHIP ARCHITECT® Suite?

☐ Yes, I would like to be on your mailing list to learn more about special offers and events.

Name _____

Title _____

Company _____

Address _____

City_____State _____ ZIP _____

Country _____

Telephone _____FAX _____

E-mail _____

I work for:
☐ A corporation
☐ A consulting organization
☐ An educational institution

Complete and FAX to: 952-345-3601

www.lominger.com

FYI For Talent Management™
The Talent Development Handbook

Robert W. Eichinger
Michael M. Lombardo
Cara Capretta Raymond

Published by Lominger Limited, Inc.
Minneapolis, MN

t are most like you (highs), and nine items that are least like you
er to Dimensions 1-27 in the book that correspond with your lows

		High	Low
15.	Interested in what people have to say; pays attention; is good at sizing up people.	☐	☐
16.	A continuous improver; actively seeks personal learning and skill building.	☐	☐
17.	Comfortable with personal change, isn't paralyzed by mistakes; seeks feedback and moves on.	☐	☐
18.	Behaves situationally; can move in many directions, play different roles, involve others or just act. Open to counter evidence.	☐	☐
19.	Candid, knows what he/she is good and lousy at, not afraid to admit it and compensate; may be seen as humble and human, but might also be seen as too revealing by some.	☐	☐
20.	Likes test cases—ideas, products, services; fiddles with things to improve something or to come up with a creative solution; comfortable trying several times before finding the right solution.	☐	☐
21.	Can manage ideas so they become practice; can move ideas to market; is both team and organizationally savvy.	☐	☐
22.	Philosophical about personal attacks; knows that people will be upset by change, negative consequences are possible; goes ahead with change.	☐	☐
23.	Introduces a different slant; good at "what ifs" and scenarios.	☐	☐
24.	Can build a team through motivation and through the confidence the team has in him/her.	☐	☐
25.	Performs well under first-time, changing or tough conditions.	☐	☐
26.	Works hard on many fronts; high standards of excellence.	☐	☐
27.	You know he/she is around; self-assured, can be passionate about beliefs.	☐	☐

Instructions

Use this fold-out form as a simple self-evaluation that can be reviewed with your boss for a developmental discussion.

Differentiate your strengths and development needs by checking the nine items th
(lows). Review your highs and lows with your boss to validate your assessment. Re
to build supporting developmental strategies.

		High	Low
1.	Very knowledgeable on a host of work and non-work topics.	☐	☐
2.	Comfortable with things that don't fit; casts a broad net; doesn't try to make things simpler than they are; can pull from many sources, see the importance of many factors.	☐	☐
3.	Intellectually rigorous; looks deeply at many sources, hunts for parallels, contrasts, unique combinations. Isn't afraid to go off on an intellectual tangent and take time to think through something.	☐	☐
4.	Takes the time to look at and question conventional wisdom; doesn't accept much as a given; looks beyond.	☐	☐
5.	Comfortable when things are up in the air; shifts gears easily.	☐	☐
6.	Looks for root causes; interested in why; good at separating the more from the less important.	☐	☐
7.	Searches for the new; curious, likes to have many things going at once.	☐	☐
8.	Ingenious problem solver; can combine parts of ideas, come up with missing pieces, play with different combinations, etc.	☐	☐
9.	Considers the audience; is articulate, can make the complex understandable; uses appropriate language to sell a view; fairly presents the arguments of others.	☐	☐
10.	Constructive with others; knows how to handle conflicts and disagreements; watches others closely and adjusts.	☐	☐
11.	Unbiased; can easily state cases he or she disagrees with like an accomplished debater; accurate, fair, others will listen to what this person says.	☐	☐
12.	Likes to see others do well; generous in credit and help.	☐	☐
13.	Uses humor well; knows how to lighten things up.	☐	☐
14.	Open to others, can change his/her mind; deals well with the differing actions and beliefs of others; open to new ideas, solutions.	☐	☐

FYI for Talent Management™

Robert W. Eichinger
Michael M. Lombardo
Cara Capretta Raymond

LOMINGER
The Leadership Architects™
w w w . l o m i n g e r . c o m